THE

AMATEUR POACHER

THE
AMATEUR POACHER

Richard Jefferies

Author of
The Gamekeeper at Home, Wild Life in a Southern County,
Greene Ferne Farm, Hodge and his Masters

EXCELLENT PRESS
LUDLOW

First published in 1879 by Smith, Elder, & Co.
Reissued in 2006 by
Excellent Press
9 Lower Raven Lane
Ludlow
Shropshire
SY8 1BW

A copy of the British Library Cataloguing in Publication Data
for this title is available from the British Library

ISBN 10: 1 900318 22 9
ISBN 13: 978 1 900318 22 8
Printed in Great Britain by
TJ International Ltd

PREFACE

——◦•◦——

THE following pages are arranged somewhat in the order of time, beginning with the first gun, and attempts at shooting. Then come the fields, the first hills, and woods explored, often without a gun, or any thought of destruction : and next the poachers, and other odd characters observed at their work. Perhaps the idea of shooting with a matchlock, or wheel-lock, might, if put in practice, at least afford some little novelty.

R. J.

CONTENTS

———◆◇◆———

THE

AMATEUR POACHER

———◆◇◆———

CHAPTER I

THE FIRST GUN

THEY burned the old gun that used to stand in the
dark corner up in the garret, close to the stuffed fox
that always grinned so fiercely. Perhaps the reason
why he seemed in such a ghastly rage was that he
did not come by his death fairly. Otherwise his pelt
would not have been so perfect. And why else
was he put away up there out of sight?—and so
magnificent a brush as he had too. But there he
stood, and mounted guard over the old flintlock that
was so powerful a magnet to us in those days. Though
to go up there alone was no slight trial of moral
courage after listening to the horrible tales of the
carters in the stable, or the old women who used to

sit under the hedge in the shade, on an armful of hay, munching their crusts at luncheon time.

The great cavernous place was full of shadows in the brightest summer day; for the light came only through the chinks in the shutters. These were flush with the floor and bolted firmly. The silence was intense, it being so near the roof and so far away from the inhabited parts of the house. Yet there were sometimes strange acoustical effects—as when there came a low tapping at the shutters, enough to make your heart stand still. There was then nothing for it but to dash through the doorway into the empty cheese-room adjoining, which was better lighted. No doubt it was nothing but the labourers knocking the stakes in for the railing round the rickyard, but why did it sound just exactly outside the shutters? When that ceased the staircase creaked, or the pear-tree boughs rustled against the window. The staircase always waited till you had forgotten all about it before the loose worm-eaten planks sprang back to their place.

Had it not been for the merry whistling of the starlings on the thatch above, it would not have been possible to face the gloom and the teeth of Reynard, ever in the act to snap, and the mystic noises, and the sense of guilt—for the gun was forbidden. Besides

which there was the black mouth of the open trapdoor
overhead yawning fearfully—a standing terror and
temptation ; for there was a legend of a pair of pistols
thrown up there out of the way—a treasure-trove tempting enough to make us face anything. But Orion must
have the credit of the courage ; I call him Orion
because he was a hunter and had a famous dog. The
last I heard of him he had just ridden through a prairie
fire, and says the people out there think nothing of it.

We dragged an ancient linen-press under the trapdoor, and put some boxes on that, and finally a
straight-backed oaken chair. One or two of those
chairs were split up and helped to do the roasting on
the kitchen hearth. So, climbing the pile, we emerged
under the rafters, and could see daylight faintly in
several places coming through the starlings' holes.
One or two bats fluttered to and fro as we groped
among the lumber, but no pistols could be discovered ;
nothing but a cannon-ball, rusty enough and about
as big as an orange, which they say was found in the
wood, where there was a brush in Oliver's time.

In the middle of our expedition there came the
well-known whistle, echoing about the chimneys, with
which it was the custom to recall us to dinner. How
else could you make people hear who might be cutting
a knobbed stick in the copse half a mile away or

bathing in the lake ? We had to jump down with a run ; and then came the difficulty ; for black dusty cobwebs, the growth of fifty years, clothed us from head to foot. There was no brushing or picking them off, with that loud whistle repeated every two minutes.

The fact where we had been was patent to all ; and so the chairs got burned—but one, which was rickety. After which a story crept out, of a disjointed skeleton lying in a corner under the thatch. Though just a little suspicious that this might be a *ruse* to frighten us from a second attempt, we yet could not deny the possibility of its being true. Sometimes in the dusk, when I sat poring over ' Kœnigsmark, the Robber,' by the little window in the cheese-room, a skull seemed to peer down the trapdoor. But then I had the flintlock by me for protection.

There were giants in the days when that gun was made ; for surely no modern mortal could have held that mass of metal steady to his shoulder. The linen-press and a chest on the top of it formed, however, a very good gun-carriage ; and, thus mounted, aim could be taken out of the window at the old mare feeding in the meadow below by the brook, and a ' bead ' could be drawn upon Molly, the dairy-maid, kissing the fogger behind the hedge, little dreaming that the deadly tube was levelled at them. At least this practice and drill had one useful effect— the eye got accustomed to the flash from the pan, instead of blinking the discharge, which ruins the shooting. Almost everybody and everything on the place got shot dead in this way without knowing it.

It was not so easy as might be supposed to find proper flints. The best time to look for them was after a heavy storm of rain had washed a shallow channel beside the road, when you might select some handy splinters which had lain hidden under the dust. How we were found out is not quite clear: perhaps the powder left a smell of sulphur for any one who chanced to go up in the garret.

But, however that may be, one day, as we came in unexpectedly from a voyage in the punt, something was discovered burning among the logs on the kitchen hearth; and, though a desperate rescue was attempted, nothing was left but the barrel of our precious gun and some crooked iron representing the remains of the lock. There are things that are never entirely forgiven, though the impression may become fainter as years go by. The sense of the cruel injustice of that act will never quite depart.

But they could not burn the barrel, and we almost succeeded in fitting it to a stock of elder. Elder has a thick pith running down the centre : by removing that the gouge and chisel had not much work to do to make a groove for the old bell-mouthed barrel to lie in. The matchlock, for as such it was intended, was nearly finished when our hopes were dashed to the ground by a piece of unnatural cunning. One morning the breechpiece that screwed in was missing. This was fatal. A barrel without a breechpiece is like a cup without a bottom. It was all over.

There are days in spring when the white clouds go swiftly past, with occasional breaks of bright sunshine lighting up a spot in the landscape. That is like the memory of one's youth. There is a long dull blank, and then a brilliant streak of recollection. Doubtless it was a year or two afterwards when, seeing that the natural instinct could not be suppressed but had better be recognised, they produced a real gun (single-barrel) for me from the clock-case.

It stood on the landing just at the bottom of the dark flight that led to the garret. An oaken case six feet high or more, and a vast dial, with a mysterious picture of a full moon and a ship in full sail that somehow indicated the quarters of the year, if you had been imitating Rip Van Winkle and after a sleep of six months wanted to know whether it was spring or autumn. But only to think that all the while we were puzzling over the moon and the ship and the queer signs on the dial a gun was hidden inside! The case was locked, it is true; but there are ways of opening locks, and we were always handy with tools.

This gun was almost, but not quite so long as the other. That dated from the time between Stuart and Hanover; this might not have been more than seventy years old. And a beautiful piece of workmanship it was: my new double breechloader is a coarse common thing to compare with it. Long and slender and light as a feather, it came to the shoulder with wonderful ease. Then there was a groove on the barrel at the breech and for some inches up which caught the eye and guided the glance like a trough to the sight at the muzzle and thence to the bird. The stock was shod with brass, and the trigger-guard was of brass, with a kind of flange stretching half-way down to the butt and inserted in the wood. After a few minutes' polishing it shone like gold, and to see the sunlight flash on it was a joy.

You might note the grain of the barrel, for it had not been browned; and it took a good deal of sand to get the rust off. By aid of a little oil and careful wiping after a shower it was easy to keep it bright. Those browned barrels only encourage idleness. The

lock was a trifle dull at first, simply from lack of use.
A small screwdriver soon had it to pieces, and it
speedily clicked again sweet as a flute. If the hammer came back rather far when at full-cock, that
was because the lock had been converted from a flint,
and you could not expect it to be absolutely perfect.
Besides which, as the fall was longer the blow was
heavier, and the cap was sure to explode.

By old farmhouses, mostly in exposed places (for
which there is a reason), one or more huge walnut
trees may be found. The provident folk of those
days planted them with the purpose of having their
own gunstocks cut out of the wood when the tree
was thrown. They could then be sure it was really
walnut, and a choice piece of timber thoroughly well
seasoned. I like to think of those times, when men
settled themselves down, and planted and planned
and laid out their gardens and orchards and woods,
as if they and their sons and sons' sons, to the twen-
tieth generation, were sure to enjoy the fruit of their
labour.

The reason why the walnuts are put in exposed
places, on the slope of a rise, with open aspect to the
east and north, is because the walnut is a foolish tree
that will not learn by experience. If it feels the
warmth of a few genial days in early spring, it imme-

diately protrudes its buds; and the next morning a
bitter frost cuts down every hope of fruit for that
year, leaving the leaf as black as may be. Wherefore
the east wind is desirable to keep it as backward as
possible.

There was a story that the stock of this gun had
been cut out of a walnut tree that was thrown on
the place by my great-grandfather, who saw it well
seasoned, being a connoisseur of timber, which is,
indeed, a sort of instinct in all his descendants. And
a vast store of philosophy there is in timber if you
study it aright.

After cleaning the gun and trying it at a mark,
the next thing was to get a good shot with it. Now
there was an elm that stood out from the hedge a
little, almost at the top of the meadow, not above
five-and-twenty yards from the other hedge that
bounded the field. Two mounds could therefore be
commanded by any one in ambush behind the elm,
and all the angular corner of the mead was within
range.

It was not far from the house; but the ground
sank into a depression there, and the ridge of it
behind shut out everything except just the roof of
the tallest hayrick. As one sat on the sward behind
the elm, with the back turned on the rick and nothing

in front but the tall elms and the oaks in the other hedge, it was quite easy to fancy it the verge of the prairie with the backwoods close by.

The rabbits had scratched the yellow sand right out into the grass—it is always very much brighter in colour where they have just been at work—and the fern, already almost yellow too, shaded the mouths of their buries. Thick bramble bushes grew out from the mound and filled the space between it and the elm : there were a few late flowers on them still, but the rest were hardening into red sour berries. Westwards, the afternoon sun, with all his autumn heat, shone full against the hedge and into the recess, and there was not the shadow of a leaf for shelter on that side.

The gun was on the turf, and the little hoppers kept jumping out of the grass on to the stock : once their king, a grasshopper, alighted on it and rested, his green limbs tipped with red rising above his back. About the distant wood and the hills there was a soft faint haze, which is what Nature finishes her pictures with. Something in the atmosphere which made it almost visible : all the trees seemed to stand in a liquid light—the sunbeams were suspended in the air instead of passing through. The butterflies even were very idle in the slumberous warmth ; and the great green dragon-fly rested on a leaf, his tail arched a little downwards, just as he puts it when he wishes to stop suddenly in his flight.

The broad glittering trigger-guard got quite hot in the sun, and the stock was warm when I felt it every now and then. The grain of the walnut-wood showed plainly through the light polish : it was not varnished like the stock of the double-barrel they kept padlocked to the rack over the high mantelpiece indoors. Still you could see the varnish. It was of a rich dark horse-chestnut colour, and yet so bright and clear that if held close you could see your face in it. Behind it the grain of the wood was just perceptible ; especially at the grip, where hard hands had worn it away somewhat. The secret of that varnish is lost—like that of the varnish on the priceless old violins.

But you could feel the wood more in my gun : so that it was difficult to keep the hand off it, though the rabbits would not come out ; and the shadowless recess grew like a furnace, for it focussed the rays of the sun. The heat on the sunny side of a thick hedge between three and four in the afternoon is almost tropical if you remain still, because the air is motionless : the only relief is to hold your hat loose ; or tilt it against your head, the other edge of the brim on

the ground.   Then the grass-blades rise up level with
the forehead.   There is a delicious smell in growing
grass, and a sweetness comes up from the earth.

Still it got hotter and hotter; and it was not
possible to move in the least degree, lest a brown
creature sitting on the sand at the mouth of his hole,
and hidden himself by the fern, should immediately
note it.   And Orion was waiting in the rickyard for
the sound of the report, and very likely the shepherd
too.   We knew that men in Africa, watched by lions,
had kept still in the sunshine till, reflected from the
rock, it literally scorched them, not daring to move;
and we knew all about the stoicism of the Red
Indians.   But Ulysses was ever my pattern and
model: that man of infinite patience and resource.

So, though the sun might burn and the air
become suffocating in that close corner, and the
quivering line of heat across the meadow make the
eyes dizzy to watch, yet not a limb must be moved.
The black flies came in crowds; but they are not so
tormenting if you plunge your face in the grass,
though they titillate the back of the hand as they run
over it.   Under the bramble bush was a bury that did
not look much used; and once or twice a great blue
fly came out of it, the buzz at first sounding hollow
and afar off and becoming clearer as it approached

the mouth of the hole. There was the carcass of a dead rabbit inside no doubt.

A humble-bee wandering along—they are restless things—buzzed right under my hat, and became entangled in the grass by my ear. Now we knew by experience in taking their honey that they could sting sharply if irritated, though good-tempered by nature. How he 'burred' and buzzed and droned !— till by-and-by, crawling up the back of my head, he found an open space and sailed away. Then, looking out again, there was a pair of ears in the grass not ten yards distant : a rabbit had come out at last. But the first delight was quickly over : the ears were short and sharply pointed, and almost pinkly transparent.

What would the shepherd say if I brought home one of his hated enemies no bigger than a rat ? The young rabbit made waiting still more painful, being far enough from the hedge to get a clear view into the recess if anything attracted his notice. Why the shepherd hated rabbits was because the sheep would not feed where they had worn their runs in the grass. Not the least movement was possible now—not even that little shifting which makes a position just endur-able : the heat seemed to increase ; the thought of Ulysses could hardly restrain the almost irresistible desire to stir.

When, suddenly, there was a slight rustling among the boughs of an oak in the other hedge, as of wings against twigs : it was a woodpigeon, better game than a rabbit. He would, I knew, first look round before he settled himself to preen his feathers on the branch, and, if everything was still while that keen inspection lasted, would never notice me. This is their habit—and the closer you are underneath them the less chance of their perceiving you : for a pigeon perched rarely looks straight downwards. If flying, it is just the reverse ; for then they seem to see under them quicker than in any other direction.

Slowly lifting the long barrel of the gun—it was fortunate the sunlight glancing on the bright barrel was not reflected towards the oak—I got it to bear upon the bird ; but then came a doubt. It was all eight-and-twenty yards across the angle of the meadow to the oak—a tremendous long shot under the circumstances. For they would not trust us with the large copper powder-flask, but only with a little pistol-flask (it had belonged to the pair of pistols we tried to find), and we were ordered not to use more than a charge and a half at a time. That was quite enough to kill blackbirds. (The noise of the report was always a check in this way ; such a trifle of powder only made a slight puff.)

Shot there was in plenty—a whole tobacco-pipe bowl full, carefully measured out of the old yellow canvas money-bag that did for a shot belt. A starling could be knocked off the chimney with this charge easily, and so could a blackbird roosting in a bush at night. But a woodpigeon nearly thirty yards distant was another matter ; for the old folk (and the birdkeepers too) said that their quills were so hard the shot would glance aside unless it came with great force. Very likely the pigeon would escape, and all the rabbits in the buries would be too frightened to come out at all.

A beautiful bird he was on the bough, perched well in view and clearly defined against the sky behind ; and my eye travelled along the groove on the breech and up the barrel, and so to the sight and across to him ; and the finger, which always would keep time with the eye, pulled at the trigger.

A mere puff of a report, and then a desperate fluttering in the tree and a cloud of white feathers floating above the hedge, and a heavy fall among the bushes. He was down, and Orion's spaniel (that came racing like mad from the rickyard the instant he heard the discharge) had him in a moment. Orion followed quickly. Then the shepherd came up, rather stiff on his legs from rheumatism, and stepped the distance, declaring it was thirty yards good ; after which we all walked home in triumph.

Molly the dairymaid came a little way from the rickyard, and said she would pluck the pigeon that very night after work. She was always ready to do anything for us boys : and we could never quite make out why they scolded her so for an idle hussy indoors. It seemed so unjust. Looking back, I recollect she had very beautiful brown eyes.

'You mind you chaws the shot well, measter,' said the shepherd, 'afore you loads th' gun. The more you chaws it the better it sticks thegither, an' the furder it kills um :' a theory of gunnery that which was devoutly believed in in his time and long anticipated the wire cartridges. And the old soldiers that used to come round to haymaking, glad of a job to supplement their pensions, were very positive that if you bit the bullet and indented it with your teeth, it was perfectly fatal, no matter to what part of the body its billet took it.

In the midst of this talk as we moved on, I carrying the gun at the trail with the muzzle downwards, the old ramrod, long disused and shrunken, slipped half out ; the end caught the ground, and it snapped short off in a second. A terrible disaster this, turning everything to bitterness : Orion was especially wroth,

for it was his right next to shoot. However, we went
down to the smithy at the inn, to take counsel of the
blacksmith, a man of knowledge and a trusty friend.
'Aha!' said he, 'it's not the first time I've made a
ramrod. There's a piece of lancewood in the store
overhead which I keep on purpose ; it's as tough as
a bow—they make carriage-shafts of it ; you shall
have a better rod than was ever fitted to a Joe
Manton.' So we took him down some pippins, and
he set to work on it that evening.

CHAPTER II

THE OLD PUNT: A CURIOUS 'TURNPIKE'

THE sculls of our punt, being short and stout, answered very well as levers to heave the clumsy old craft off the sand into which it sank so deeply. That sheltered corner of the mere, with a shelving sandy shore, and a steep bank behind covered with trees, was one of the best places to fish for roach : you could see them playing under the punt in shoals any sunny day.

There was a projecting bar almost enclosing the creek, which was quite still, even when the surf whitened the stony strand without, driven before a wet and stormy south-wester. It was the merest routine to carry the painter ashore and twist the rotten rope round an exposed root of the great willow tree ; for there was not the slightest chance of that ancient craft breaking adrift.

All our strength and the leverage of the sculls

could scarcely move her, so much had she settled. But we had determined to sail that lovely day to visit the island of Calypso, and had got all our arms and munitions of war aboard, besides being provisioned and carrying some fruit for fear of scurvy. There was of course the gun, placed so as not to get wet; for the boat leaked, and had to be frequently baled out with a tin mug—one that the haymakers used.

Indeed, if we had not caulked her with some dried moss and some stiff clay, it is doubtful if she would have floated far. The well was full of dead leaves that had been killed by the caterpillars and the blight, and had fallen from the trees before their time; and there were one or two bunches of grass growing at the stern part from between the decaying planks.

Besides the gun there was the Indian bow, scooped out inside in a curious way, and covered with strange designs or coloured hieroglyphics: it had been brought home by one of our people years before. There was but one man in the place who could bend that bow effectually; so that though we valued it highly we could not use it. By it lay another of briar, which was pliable enough and had brought down more than one bird.

Orion hit a rabbit once; but though sore wounded

it got to the bury, and, struggling in, the arrow caught
the side of the hole and was drawn out.   Indeed, a
nail filed sharp is not of much avail as an arrowhead ;
you must have it barbed, and that was a little
beyond our skill.   Ikey the blacksmith had forged us
a spearhead after a sketch from a picture of a Greek
warrior ; and a rake-handle served as a shaft.   It was
really a dangerous weapon.   He had also made us
a small anchor according to plan ; nor did he dip too
deeply into our pocket-money.

Then the mast and square-sail, fitted out of a
window-blind, took up a considerable space ; for
although it was perfectly calm, a breeze might arise.
And what with these and the pole for punting occasionally, the deck of the vessel was in that approve
state of confusion which always characterises a ship
on the point of departure.   Nor must Orion's fishing-
rod and gear be forgotten, nor the cigar-box at the
stern (a present from the landlady at the inn) which
contained a chart of the mere and a compass.

With a 'yeo—heave-ho !' we levered her an inch
at a time, and then loosened her by working her from
side to side, and so, panting and struggling, shoved
the punt towards the deep.   Slowly a course was
shaped out of the creek—past the bar and then
along the edge of the thick weeds, stretching so far

out into the water that the moorhen feeding near the land was beyond reach of shot. From the green matted mass through which a boat could scarcely have been forced came a slight uncertain sound, now here now yonder, a faint 'suck-sock;' and the dragon-flies were darting to and fro.

The only ripple of the surface, till broken by the sculls, was where the swallows dipped as they glided, leaving a circle of tiny wavelets that barely rolled a yard. Past the low but steep bluff of sand rising sheer out of the water, drilled with martins' holes and topped by a sapling oak in the midst of a great furze bush : yellow bloom of the furze, tall brake fern nestling under the young branches, woodbine climbing up and bearing sweet coronals of flower.

Past the barley that came down to the willows by the shore—ripe and white under the bright sunshine, but yonder beneath the shadow of the elms with a pale tint of amber. Past broad rising meadows, where under the oaks on the upper ground the cattle were idly lying out of the sultry heat.

Then the barren islands, strewn with stone and mussel-shells glistening in the sunshine, over which in a gale the waves made a clean sweep, rendered the navigation intricate ; and the vessel had to be worked in and out, now scraping against rocky walls of sandstone, now grounding and churning up the bottom, till presently she floated in the bay beneath the firs. There a dark shadow hung over the black water—still and silent, so still that even the aspens rested from their rustling.

Out again into the sunshine by the wide mouth of the Green River, as the chart named the brook whose level stream scarce moved into the lake. A streak of blue shot up it between the banks, and a shrill pipe came back as the kingfisher hastened away. By the huge boulder of sarsen, whose shoulder projected but a few inches—in stormy times a dangerous rock to mariners—and then into the unknown narrow seas between the endless osier-beds and withy-covered isles.

There the chart failed ; and the known landmarks across the open waters—the firs and elms, the green knoll with the cattle—were shut out by thick branches on either hand. In and out and round the islets, sounding the depth before advancing, winding now this way, now that, till all idea of the course was lost, and it became a mere struggle to get forward. Drooping boughs swept along the gunwales, thick-matted weeds cumbered the way ; 'snags,' jagged stumps of trees, threatened to thrust their tops through the bottom ; and, finally, panting and weary of poling through the maze, we emerged in a narrow creek all walled in and enclosed with vegetation.

Running her ashore on the soft oozy ground, we rested under a great hawthorn bush that grew at the very edge, and, looking upwards, could see in the canopy above the black interlaced twigs of a dove's nest. Tall willow poles rose up all around, and above them was the deep blue of the sky. On the willow stems that were sometimes under water the bark had peeled in scales; beneath the surface bunches of red fibrous roots stretched out their slender filaments tipped with white, as if feeling like a living thing for prey.

A dreamy, slumberous place, where the sedges slept, and the green flags bowed their pointed heads. Under the bushes in the distant nook the moorhen, reassured by the silence, came out from the grey-green grass and the rushes. Surely Calypso's cave could not be far distant, where she with

> work and song the time divides,
> And through the loom the golden shuttle guides.

For the Immortals are hiding somewhere still in the woods ; even now I do not weary searching for them.

But as we rested a shadow fell from a cloud that covered the sun, and immediately a faint sigh arose from among the sedges and the reeds, and two pale yellow leaves fell from the willows on the water.

A gentle breeze followed the cloud, chasing its shadow. Orion touched his rod meaningly.

So I stepped ashore with the gun to see if a channel could be found into the open water, and pushed through the bush. Briar and bramble choked the path, and hollow willow stoles; but, holding the gun upright, it was possible to force through, till, pushing between a belt of reeds and round an elder thicket, I came suddenly on a deep, clear pool—all but walking into it. Up rose a large bird out of the water with a bustling of wings and splashing, compelled to 'rocket' by the thick bushes and willow poles. There was no time to aim; but the old gun touched the shoulder and went off without conscious volition on my part.

The bird flew over the willows, but the next moment there was a heavy splash somewhere beyond out of sight. Then came an echo of the report sent back from the woods adjoining, and another, and a third and fourth, as the sound rolled along the side of the hill, caught in the coombes and thrown to and fro like a ball in a tennis-court. Wild with anxiety, we forced the punt at the bulrushes, in the corner where it looked most open, and with all our might heaved it over the weeds and the mud, and so round the islet into the next pool, and thence into the open water. It was a wild duck, and was speedily on board.

Stepping the mast and hoisting the sail, we drifted before the faint breath of air that now just curled the surface, steering straight across the open for the stony barren islands at the mouth of the bay. The chart drawn in pencil—what labour it cost us! —said that there, a few yards from the steep shore, was a shoal with deep water round it. For some reason there always seemed a slight movement or current—a set of the water there, as if it flowed into the little bay.

In swimming we often came suddenly out of a cold into a stratum of warm water (at the surface); and perhaps the difference in the temperature may have caused the drift, for the bay was in shadow half the day. Now, wherever there is motion there will fish assemble; so as the punt approached the shoal the sail was doused, and at twenty yards' distance I *put* the anchor into the water—not dropping it, to avoid the splash—and let it slip gently to the bottom.

Then, paying out the cable, we drifted to the edge of the shoal without the least disturbance, and there brought up. Orion had his bait ready—he threw his line right to windward, so that the float might drag the worm naturally with the wind and slight current towards the shoal.

The tiny blue buoy dances up and down on the miniature waves ; beyond it a dazzling path of gold stretches away to the distant osier-islands—a path down which we came without seeing it till we looked back. The wavelets strike with a faint 'sock-sock' against the bluff overhanging bow, and then roll on to the lee-shore close at hand.

It rises steep ; then a broad green ledge ; and after that, still steeper, the face of a long-deserted sandpit, where high up a rabbit sits at the mouth of his hole, within range, but certain to escape even if hit, and therefore safe. On the turf below is a round black spot, still showing, though a twelvemonth has gone by since we landed with half a dozen perch, lit a fire and cooked the fishes. For Molly never could 'a-bear' perch, because of the hardness of the scales, saying she would as soon 'scrape a vlint ;' and they laughed to scorn our idea of skinning them as you do moorhens, whose 'dowl' no fingers can pick.

So we lit a fire and blew it up, lying on the soft short grass in a state of nature after a swim, there being none to see us but the glorious sun. The skinned perch were sweeter than any I have tasted since.

'Look! whispers Orion, suddenly. The quill above the blue buoy nods as it lifts over the wavelets —nods again, sinks a little, jerks up, and then goes down out of sight. Orion feels the weight. 'Two pounds, if he's an ounce!' he shouts: soon after a splendid perch is in the boat, nearer three pounds perhaps than two. Flop! whop! how he leaps up and down on the planks, soiled by the mud, dulling his broad back and barred sides on the grit and sand.

Roaming about like this with the gun, now on the water in the punt, and now on land, we gradually came to notice very closely the game we wished to shoot. We saw, for instance, that the rabbit when feeding or moving freely, unless quickened by alarm, has a peculiar way of dwelling upon his path. It almost resembles creeping; for both fore feet stop while the hinder come up—one hinder foot slightly behind the other, and rather wide apart.

When a fall of snow presents a perfect impression of his passage, it appears as if the animal had walked slowly backwards. This deceives many who at such times go out to pick up anything that comes in their way; for they trace the trail in the wrong direction. The truth is, that when the rabbit pauses for the hinder feet to come up he again rests momentarily

upon these before the two foremost are put forth, and
so presses not only the paw proper but the whole first
joint of the hind leg upon the snow. A glance at the
hind feet of a rabbit will show what I mean : they will
be found to display plain signs of friction against the
ground.

The habit has given the creature considerable
power of standing up on the hinder feet ; he can not
only sit on his haunches, but raise himself almost upright, and remain in that position to listen for some
little time. For the same reason he can bark the ash
saplings higher up than would be imagined : where he
cannot reach, the mice climb up and nibble straight
lines across the young pole, as if done with a single
stroke from a saw that scraped away the rind but
did not reach the wood.

In front of a large rabbit bury the grass will be
found discoloured with sand at some distance from
the mouth of the hole. This is explained by particles
adherent to the rabbits' hind feet, and rubbing off
against the grass blades. Country people call this
peculiar gait 'sloppetting ;' and one result of it is
that the rabbits wear away the grass where they are
numerous almost as much as they eat it away.

There was such a space worn by the attrition of
feet sprinkled with sand before the extensive burrow

at the top of the meadow where I shot the wood-pigeon. These marks suggested to us that we should attempt some more wholesale system of capture than shooting. It was not for the mere desire of destruction, but for a special purpose, that we turned our attention to wiring. The punt, though much beloved, was, like all punts, a very bad sailer. A boat with a keel that could tack, and so work into the wind's eye, was our ambition.

The blacksmith Ikey readily purchased every rabbit we obtained at sixpence each. Rabbits were not so dear then as now ; but of course he made a large profit even then. The same rabbits at present would be worth fifteen or eighteen pence. Every sixpence was carefully saved, but it was clear that a long time must elapse before the goal was attained. The blacksmith started the idea of putting up a 'turn-pike '—*i.e.* a wire—but professed ignorance as to the method of setting it. That was a piece of his cunning —that he might escape responsibility.

The shepherd, too, when obliquely questioned, shook his head, pursed his lips, threw his pitching-bar over his shoulder, and marched off with a mysterious hint that our friend Ikey would some day put his 'vut in it.' It did not surprise us that the shepherd should turn his back on anything of the kind ; for he was a leading man among the 'Ranters,' and frequently exhorted them in his cottage.

The carter's lad was about at the time, and for the moment we thought of applying to him. He was standing on the threshold of the stable, under the horseshoes and weasels' feet nailed up to keep the witches away, teasing a bat that he had found under the tiles. But suddenly the dusky thing bit him sharply, and he uttered an oath; while the creature, released, flew aimlessly into the elms. It was better to avoid him.

Indoors, they would have put a very heavy hand upon the notion had they known of it : so we had to rely solely upon the teaching of experiment. In the first attempt, a stick that had been put by for the thatcher, but which he had not yet split, was cut short and sharpened for the plug that prevents the animal carrying away the wire when snared. This is driven into the earth ; at the projecting end a notch was cut to hold the string attached to the end of the wire away from the run.

A smaller stick supported the wire above the ground; this latter only just sufficiently thrust into the sward to stand firmly upright. Willow was used for this at first ; but it is a feeble wood : it split too much, or bent and gave way instead of hold-

ing the wire in its place. The best for the purpose
we found were the nut-tree rods that shoot up among
the hazel thickets, no larger than the shaft of an arrow,
and almost as straight. A slit about half an inch deep
was made in the upper end, and in this slit the shank
of the wire was sunk. Once or twice the upright
was peeled; but this was a mistake, for the white
wand was then too conspicuous. The bark should
be left on.

Three copper wires twisted tight formed the snare
itself; we twisted them like the strands of a rope,
thinking it would give more strength. The wire projected horizontally, the loop curling downwards. It
was first set up at a spot where a very broad and
much-worn run—more like a footpath than a rabbit
track—forked into several lesser runs, and at about
five yards from the hedge. But though adjusted, as
we thought, with the utmost nicety, no rabbit would
put his neck into it—not even in the darkness of the
night. By day they all played round it in perfect
safety.

After waiting some time it was removed and reset
just over a hole—the loop close to the opening. It
looked scarcely possible for a rabbit to creep out
without being caught, the loop being enlarged to cor-
respond with the mouth of the hole. For a while it

seemed as if the rabbits declined to use the hole at
all; presently, however, the loop was pushed back,
showing that one must have got his nose between it
and the bank and so made a safe passage sideways.
A run that crossed the field was then selected, and the
wire erected at about the middle of it, equidistant from
either hedge. Near the entrance of the buries the
rabbits moved slowly, sniffing their way along and
pausing every yard or so. But they often increased
their speed farther away, and sometimes raced from
one mound to the other. When going at that rate it
appeared natural to conclude that they would be less
careful to pick and choose their road.

The theory proved so far correct that next day
the upright was down, but the wire had snapped and
the rabbit was gone. The character of the fracture
clearly indicated how it had happened: the rabbit, so
soon as he found his head in the noose, had rolled and
tumbled till the wire, already twisted tight, parted.
Too much twisting, therefore, weakened instead of
strengthening. Next a single wire, somewhat thicker,
was used, and set up nearly in the same place; but it
broke again.

Finally, two strands of medium size, placed side
by side, but only twisted once—that is, just enough
to keep them together—were employed. The lesser

loop—the slip-knot, as it might be called—was at the same time eased in order to run quicker and take a closer grip. Experiments with the hand proved that this style of wire would bear a great strain, and immediately answered to a sudden jerk. The running noose slipped the more easily because the wires were smooth ; when twisted the strands checked the noose, the friction causing a slight sound. The wire itself seemed nearly perfect ; but still no rabbit was caught.

Various runs were tried in succession ; the size of the loop, too, was now enlarged and now decreased ; for once it seemed as if a rabbit's ears had struck it aside, and on another as if, the loop being too large or too low down, one of the fore feet had entered and drawn it. Had it been the hind leg the noose would have held, because of the crook of the leg ; but the forefoot came through, leaving the noose drawn up to a size not much larger than a finger-ring. To decide the point accurately, a full-grown rabbit was shot, and Orion held it in a position as near as possible to that taken in running, while I adjusted the wire to fit exactly. Still no success.

At last the secret was revealed by a hare. One day, walking up the lane with the gun, and peeping over into the ploughed field, I saw a hare about sixty yards away. The distance was too great to risk a shot, or rather it was preferable to wait for the chance of his coming nearer. Stepping back gently behind the bushes, I watched him run to and fro, gradually approaching in a zig-zag line that must carry him right across in front. I was positive that he had not seen me, and felt sure of bagging him ; when suddenly— without any apparent cause—up went his head, he glanced round, and was off like the wind.

Yet there had not been the faintest noise, and I could not understand it, till all at once it occurred to me that it must be the scent. The slight, scarcely perceptible, breeze blew in that direction : instantly he crossed the current from me he detected it and fled. Afterwards I noticed that in the dusky twilight, if the wind is behind him, a hare will run straight at you as if about to deliberately charge your legs. This incident by the ploughed field explained the failure of the wire. Every other care had been taken, but we had forgotten to allow for the extreme delicacy of a wild animal's sense of smell.

In walking to the spot selected for the snare it is best to avoid even stepping on the run, and while setting it up to stand back as far as convenient and lean forward. The grass that grows near must not be touched by the hand, which seems to impart a very strong scent. The stick that has been carried in the hand must not be allowed to fall across the run : and be careful that your handkerchief does not drop out of your pocket on or near it. If a bunch of grass grows very tall and requires parting, part it with the end (not the handle) of your stick.

The same holds good with gins, especially if piaced for a rat. Some persons strew a little freshly plucked grass over the pan and teeth of the trap, thinking to hide it ; but it not only smells of the hand, but withers up and turns brown, and acts as a warning to that wary creature. It is a better plan if any dead leaves are lying near to turn them over and over with the end of a twig till they fall on the trap, that is if they are dry : if wet (unless actually raining at the time), should one chance to be left with the drier under surface uppermost, the rat may pause on the brink.

Now that the remotest chance of leaving a scent was avoided the wire became a deadly instrument. Almost every morning two or three rabbits were taken : we set up a dozen snares when we had mastered the trick. They were found lying at full length in the crisp white grass, for we often rose to visit the wires while yet the stars were visible. Thus extended a person might have passed within a few yards and never noticed them, unless he had an out-of-doors eye ; for the whiter fur of the belly as they lay aside was barely distinguishable from the hoar frost. The blacksmith Ikey sauntered down the lane every evening, and glanced casually behind the ash tree—the northern side of whose trunk was clothed with dark green velvet-like moss—to see if a bag was lying for him there among the nettles in the ditch. The rabbits were put in the bag, which was pushed through the hedge.

CHAPTER III

TREE-SHOOTING : A FISHING EXPEDITION

JUST on the verge and borderland of the territory
that could be ranged in safety there grew a stunted
oak in a mound beside the brook. Perhaps the roots
had been checked by the water ; for the tree, instead
of increasing in bulk, had expended its vigour in
branches so crooked that they appeared entangled in
each other. This oak was a favourite perching-place,
because of its position : it could also be more easily
climbed than straight-grown timber, having many
boughs low down the trunk. With a gun it is difficult
to ascend a smooth tree ; these boughs therefore were
a great advantage.

One warm afternoon late in the summer I got up
into this oak ; and took a seat astride a large limb, with
the main trunk behind like the back of a chair and
about twenty feet above the mound. Some lesser
branches afforded a fork on which the gun could be

securely lodged, and a limb of considerable size came across in front.   Leaning both arms on this, a view could be obtained below and on three sides easily and without effort.

The mound immediately beneath was grown over with thick blackthorn, a species of cover that gives great confidence to game.   A kick or blow upon the bushes with a stick will not move anything in an old blackthorn thicket.   A man can scarcely push through it : nothing but a dog can manage to get about.   On the meadow side there was no ditch, only a narrow fringe of tall pointed grass and rushes, with one or two small furze bushes projecting out upon the sward. Behind such bushes, on the slope of the mound, is rather a favourite place for a rabbit to sit out, or a hare to have a form.

The brook was shallow towards the hedge, and bordered with flags, among which rose up one tall bunch of beautiful reeds.   Some little way up the brook a pond opened from it.   At the entrance the bar of mud had hardly an inch of water ; within there was a clear small space, and the rest all weeds, with moorhens' tracks.   The farther side of the pond was covered with bramble bushes.   It is a good plan to send the dogs into bushes growing on the banks of ponds ; for though rabbits dislike water itself they are fond of sitting out in such cover near it. A low railing enclosed the side towards me : the posts had slipped by the giving way of the soil, and hung over the still pool.

One of the rails—of willow—was eaten out into hollow cavities by the wasps, which came to it generation after generation for the materials of their nests. The particles they detach are formed into a kind of paste or paper : in time they will quite honeycomb a pole. The third side of the pond shelved to the ' leaze,' that the cattle might drink. From it a narrow track went across the broad field up the rising ground to the distant gateway leading to the meadows, where they grazed on the aftermath. Marching day by day, one after the other in single file, to the drinking-place, the hoofs of the herd had cut a clean path in the turf, two or three inches deep and trodden hard. The reddish soil thus exposed marked the winding line athwart the field, through the tussocky bunches.

By the pond stood a low three-sided merestone or landmark, the initials on which were hidden under moss. Up in the tree, near the gun, there was a dead branch that had decayed in the curious manner that seems peculiar to oak. Where it joined the trunk the bark still remained, though covered with lichen, and for a foot or so out; then there was a long space where the bark and much of the wood had mouldered away; finally, near the end the bough retained its original size and the bark adhered. At the junction with the trunk and at the extremity its diameter was perhaps three inches; in the middle rather less than half as much. The grey central piece, larger and darker at either end, suggested the thought of the bare neck of a vulture.

Far away, just rising above the slope of the leaze, the distant tops of elms, crowded with rooks' nests (not then occupied), showed the site of the residence of an old gentleman of whom at that time we stood in much fear. The 'Squire' of Southlands alarmed even the hardened carters' lads as much by the prestige of a singular character as by the chastisement he personally gave those who ventured into his domain. Not a bird's nest, not a nut, must be touched: still less anything that could be called game. The watch kept was so much the stricter because he took a personal part in it, and was often round the fields himself armed with a great oak staff. It seemed, indeed, as if the preservation of the game was of far greater importance to him than the shooting of it afterwards. All the fowls of the air flocked to Southlands, as if it had been a refuge; yet it was not a large estate. Into the forest we had been, but Southlands was a mystery, a forbidden garden of delight, with the terror of an oaken staff (and unknown penalties) turning this way and that. Therefore the stunted old oak on the verge—the moss-grown mere-stone by the pond marked the limit—was so favourite a perching-place.

That beautiful afternoon I leaned both arms idly on the great bough that crossed in front of the seat and listened to the ' Caw—caw ! ' of the rooks as they looked to see if the acorns were yet ripening. A dead branch that had dropped partly into the brook was swayed continually up and down by the current, the water as it chafed against it causing a delicious murmur. This lulled me to sleep.

I woke with a start, and had it not been for the bough crossing in front must have fallen twenty feet. Looking down into the meadow as soon as my eyes were thoroughly open, I instantly noticed a covey of young partridges a little way up beside the hedge among the molehills. The neighbourhood of those hillocks has an attraction for many birds ; especially in winter. Then fieldfares, redwings, starlings, and others prefer the meadows that are dotted with them. In a frost if you see a thrush on a molehill it is very likely to thaw shortly. Moles seem to feel the least

change in the temperature of the earth ; if it slackens
they begin to labour, and cast up, unwittingly, food
for the thrushes.

It would have been easy to kill three or four of
the covey, which was a small one, at a single shot ;
but it had been a late summer, and they were not
full-grown.   Besides which, they roosted, I knew,
about the middle of the meadow, and to shoot them
near the roost would be certain to break them up,
and perhaps drive them into Southlands.   ' Good
poachers preserve their own game : ' so the birds fed
safely, though a pot shot would not have seemed the
crime then that it would now.   While I watched them
suddenly the old bird 'quat,' and ran swiftly into the
hedge, followed by the rest.   A kestrel was hovering
in the next meadow :   when the beat of his wings
ceased he slid forward and downwards, then rose and
came over me in a bold curve.   Well those little brown
birds in the blackthorn knew that, fierce as he was,
he dared not swoop even on a comparatively open
bush, much less such thick covert, for fear of ruffling
his proud feathers and beating them out.   Nor could
he follow them through the intricate hidden passages.

In the open water of the pond a large jack was
basking in the sunshine, just beneath the surface ;
and though the shot would scatter somewhat before

reaching him, he was within range. If a fish lies a few inches under water he is quite safe from shot unless the muzzle of the gun is so close that the pellets travel together like a bullet. At a distance the shot is supposed to glance as it strikes the water at an angle ; for that reason the elevation of the tree was an advantage, since from it the charge would plunge into the pool. A jack may be killed in some depth of water when the gun is nearly perpendicularly above the mark ; but in any case the aim must be taken two inches or more, according to circumstances, beneath the apparent position of the fish, to allow for refraction.

Sometimes the jack when hit comes to the surface belly upwards, but sometimes keeps down or sinks, and floats a considerable distance away from the spot ; so that in the muddy water disturbed by the shot it is difficult to find him. If a snake be shot at while swimming he will sometimes sink like a stone, and can be seen lying motionless at the bottom. After we got hold of a small deer rifle we used to practise at the snakes in the mere—aiming at the head, which is about the size of a nut, and shows above the surface wobbling as they move. I recollect cutting a snake's head clean off with a ball from a pistol as he hastened away through the grass.

In winter, when the jacks came up and lay immediately under the ice, they could be easily shot. The pellets cut a round hole through an inch and a half of ice. The jack now basking in the pond was the more tempting because we had often tried to wire him in vain. The difficulty was to get him if hit. While I was deliberating a crow came flying low down the leaze, and alighted by the pond. His object, no doubt, was a mussel. He could not have seen me, and yet no sooner did he touch the ground than he looked uneasily about, sprang up, and flew straight away, as if he had smelt danger. Had he stayed he would have been shot, though it would have spoiled my ambush : the idea of the crows picking out the eyes of dying creatures was always peculiarly revolting to me.

If the pond was a haunt of his, it was too near the young partridges, which were weakly that season. A kestrel is harmless compared to a crow. Surely the translators have wrongly rendered Don Quixote's remark that the English did not kill crows, believing that King Arthur, instead of dying, was by enchantment turned into one, and so fearing to injure the hero. Must he not have meant a rook ? [1]

Soon afterwards something moved out of the mound into the meadow a long distance up : it was a

[1] It has since been pointed out to me that the Don may have meant a raven.

hare. He came slowly along beside the hedge to-wards me—now stopping and looking into it as if seeking a convenient place for a form, having doubt-less been disturbed from that he had first chosen. It was some minutes before he came within range : had I been on the ground most likely he would have scented me, the light air going that way ; but being in the tree the wind that passed went high over him. For this reason a tree ambush is deadly. It was necessary to get the line of sight clear of twigs, which check and divert shot, and to take a steady aim ; for I had no second barrel, no dog, and had to descend the tree before running. Some leaves were blackened by the flame : the hare simply fell back, stretched his hind legs, quivered, and lay still. Part of the leaf of a plant was fixed in his teeth ; he had just had a nibble.

With this success I was satisfied that day ; but the old oak was always a favourite resort, even when nothing particular was in hand. From thence, too, as a base of operations, we made expeditions varying in their object with the season of the year.

Some distance beyond the stunted oak the thick blackthorn hedge was succeeded by a continuous strip of withy-bed bordering the brook. It often occurred to us that by entering these withies it would be possible to reconnoitre one side of Southlands ; for the stream skirted the lower grounds : the tall willows would conceal any one passing through them. So one spring morning the attempt was made.

It was necessary to go on hands and knees through the mowing grass for some yards while passing an open space where the blackthorn cover ended, and then to leap a broad ditch that divided the withy-beds from the meadow. The lissom willow wands parted easily and sprang back to their places behind, leaving scarce a trace. Their slender tops rose overhead ; beneath, long dead grasses, not yet quite supplanted by the spring growth, filled the space between. These rustled a little under foot, but so faint a sound could scarcely have been audible outside ; and had any one noticed it it would have been attributed to a hare or a fox moving : both are fond of lying in withy-beds when the ground is dry.

The way to walk noiselessly is to feel with the foot before letting your weight press on it ; then the dead stick or fallen hemlock is discovered and avoided. A dead stick cracks ; the dry hollow hemlock gives a splintering sound when crushed. These old hemlock stems were numerous in places, together with 'gicksies,' as the haymakers call a plant that resembles it, but has a ribbed or fluted instead of a smooth stalk. The

lads use a long 'gicks' cut between the joints as a
tube to blow haws or peggles at the girls. When
thirsty, and no ale is handy, the men search for one
to suck up water with from the brook. It is difficult
to find one free from insects, which seem to be remarkably fond of anything hollow. The haymakers
do not use the hemlock, thinking it would poison the
water ; they think, too, that drinking through a tube
is safer when they are in a great heat from the sun
than any other way.

Nor is it so easy to drink from a stream without
this simple aid. If the bank be flat it is wet, and what
looks like the grass of the meadow really grows out
of the water ; so that there it is not possible to lie at
full length. If the bank be dry the level of the water
is several inches lower, and in endeavouring to drink
the forehead is immersed ; often the water is so much
lower than its banks that it is quite impossible to drink
from it lying. By the edge grasses, water-plantains,
forget-me-nots, frequently fill the space within reach.
If you brush these aside it disturbs the bottom, and
the mud rises, or a patch of brown 'scum' comes up
and floats away. A cup, though gently used, generally draws some insects in with the water, though the
liquid itself be pure. Lapping with the hollowed
palm requires practice, and, unless the spot be free

from weeds and of some little depth, soon disturbs the bottom. But the tube can be inserted in the smallest clear place, and interferes with nothing.

Each of us carried a long hazel rod, and the handle of a 'squailer' projected from Orion's coat-pocket. For making a 'squailer' a teacup was the best mould : the cups then in use in the country were rather larger than those at present in fashion. A ground ash sapling with the bark on, about as thick as the little finger, pliant and tough, formed the shaft, which was about fifteen inches long. This was held upright in the middle of a teacup, while the mould was filled with molten lead. It soon cooled, and left a heavy conical knob on the end of the stick. If rightly thrown it was a deadly missile, and would fly almost as true as a rifle ball. A rabbit or leveret could thus be knocked over; and it was peculiarly adapted for fetching a squirrel out of a tree, because, being so heavy at one end, it rarely lodged on the boughs, as an ordinary stick would, but overbalanced and came down.

From the outlook of the oak some aspen trees could be seen far up in the withy-beds ; and it had been agreed that there the first essay of the stream should be made. On arriving at these trees we paused, and began to fix the wires on the hazel rods. The wire for fish must slip very easily, and the thinner it is, if strong enough, the better, because it takes a firmer grip. A single wire will do ; but two thin ones are preferable. Thin copper wire is as flexible as thread. Brass wire is not so good ; it is stiffer, and too conspicuous in the water.

At the shank end a stout string is attached in the middle of its length. Then the wire is placed against the rod, lying flat upon it for about six inches. The strings are now wound round tightly in opposite directions, binding it to the stick, so that at the top the ends cross and are in position to tie in the slight notch cut for the purpose. A loop that will allow four fingers to enter together is about large enough, though of course it must be varied according to the size of the jack in view. Heavy jacks are not often wired, and scarcely ever in brooks.

For jack the shape of the loop should be circular ; for trout it should be oval, and considerably larger in proportion to the apparent bulk of the fish. Jack are straight-grown and do not thicken much in the middle ; with trout it is different. The noose should be about six inches from the top of the rod. Orion said he would go twenty yards farther up ; I went direct from the centre of the withy-bed to the stream.

The bank rose a little above the level of the withy-bed ; it was a broad mound full of ash stoles

and willow—the sort that is grown for poles. At
that spot the vines of wild hops had killed all
the underwood, leaving open spaces between the
stoles ; the vines were matted so thickly that they
hid the ground.   This was too exposed a place, so I
went back and farther up till I could just hear Orion
rustling through the hemlocks.   Here the dead grass
and some elder bushes afforded shelter, and the water
could be approached unseen.

It was about six or eight inches deep ; the opposite shore was bordered for several yards out with
flags and rushes.   The cattle nibbled their tender
tops off, as far as they could reach ; farther out they
were pushing up straight and pointed.   The rib and
groove of the flag so closely resemble those of the
ancient bayonet that it might be supposed the weapon
was modelled from the plant.   Indoors among the
lumber there was a rusty old bayonet that immediately called forth the comparison : the modern make
seem more triangular.

The rushes grew nearer the shore of the meadow
—the old ones yellow, the young green : in places this
fringe of rush and sedge and flag must have been five
or six yards wide, and it extended as far as could be
seen up the brook.   No doubt the cattle trod in the
edge of the firm ground by degrees every year to get

at the water, and thus widened the marsh. It was easy to understand now why all the water-fowl, teal and duck, moorhen and snipe, seemed in winter to make in this direction.

The ducks especially exercised all our ingenuity and quite exhausted our patience in the effort to get near them in winter. In the large water-meadows a small flock sometimes remained all day: it was possible to approach near enough by stalking behind the hedges to see the colour of the mallards; but they were always out of gunshot. This place must be full of teal then; as for moorhens, there were signs of them everywhere, and several feeding in the grass. The thought of the sport to be got here when the frosty days came was enough to make one wild.

After a long look across, I began to examine the stream near at hand: the rushes and flags had forced the clear sweet current away from the meadow, so that it ran just under the bank. I was making out the brown sticks at the bottom, when there was a slight splash—caused by Orion about ten yards farther up—and almost at the same instant something shot down the brook towards me. He had doubtless landed a jack, and its fellow rushed away. Under a large dead bough that had fallen across its top in the

stream I saw the long slender fish lying a few feet
from the bank, motionless save for the gentle curving
wave of the tail edges. So faint was that waving curl
that it seemed caused rather by the flow of the
current than the volition of the fish. The wings of
the swallow work the whole of the longest summer
day, but the fins of the fish in running water are
never still : day and night they move continuously.

By slow degrees I advanced the hazel rod, keeping it at first near to and parallel with the bank,
because jack do not like anything that stretches
across them ; and I imagine other fish have the same
dislike to right angles. The straight shadow even
seems to arouse suspicion—no boughs are ever
straight. Perhaps, if it were possible to angle without a rod, there would be more success, particularly in
small streams. But after getting the stick almost out
far enough, it became evident that the dead branch
would not let me slip the wire into the water in front
of the jack in the usual way. So I had to draw it
back again as gradually as it had been put forth.

With fish everything must be done gradually and
without a jerk. A sudden, jerking movement immediately alarms them. If you walk gently by they
remain still, but start or lift the arm quickly and they
dart for deep water. The object of withdrawing the

rod was to get at and enlarge the loop in order that it might be slipped over his tail, since the head was protected by the bough. It is a more delicate operation to pass the wire up from behind ; it has to go farther before the spot that allows a firm grip is reached, and fish are well aware that natural objects such as twigs float down with the current. Anything, therefore, approaching from behind or rubbing upwards is suspicious. As this fish had just been startled, it would not do to let the wire touch him at all.

After enlarging the loop I put the rod slowly forth again, worked the wire up stream, slipped the noose over his tail, and gently got it up to the balance of the fish. Waiting a moment to get the elbow over the end of the rod so as to have a good leverage, I gave a sudden jerk upwards, and felt the weight instantly. But the top of the rod struck the overhanging bough, and there was my fish, hung indeed, but still in the water near the surface. Nor could I throw it on the bank, because of the elder bushes. So I shortened the rod, pulling it in towards me quickly and dragging the jack through the water. The pliant wire had cut into the scales and skin—he might have been safely left suspended over the stream all day ; but in the eagerness of the moment I was not satisfied till I had him up on the mound.

We did not see much of Southlands, because the withy-beds were on the lowest ground ; but there were six jacks strung on a twisted withy when we got back to the stunted oak and rested there tasting acid sorrel leaves.

CHAPTER IV

EGG-TIME. A 'GIP'-TRAP

THERE is no sweeter time in the woods than just before the nesting begins in earnest. Is it the rising sap that causes a pleasant odour to emanate from every green thing? Idling along the hedgerows towards the woodlands there may perchance be seen small tufts of white rabbit's fur in the grass, torn from herself by the doe to form a warm lining to the hole in which her litter will appear: a 'sign' this that often guides a robber to her nest.

Yonder on the rising ground, towering even in their fall over the low (lately cut) ash plantation, lie the giant limbs of the mighty oaks, thrown just as they felt the quickening heat. The bark has been stripped from the trunk and branches; the sun has turned the exposed surface to a deep buff colour, which contrasts with the fresh green of the underwood around and renders them visible afar.

When the oak first puts forth its buds the woods take a ruddy tint. Gradually the background of green comes to the front, and the oak-apples swell, streaked with rosy stains, whence their semblance to the edible fruit of the orchard. All unconscious of the white or red cross daubed on the rough bark, the tree prepares its glory of leaf, though doomed the while by that sad mark to the axe.

Cutting away the bushes with his billhook, the woodman next swings the cumbrous grub-axe, whose wide edge clears the earth from the larger roots. Then he puts his pipe in his pocket, and settles to the serious work of the 'great axe,' as he calls it. I never could use this ungainly tool aright: a top-heavy, clumsy, awkward thing, it rules you instead of you ruling it. The handle, too, is flat—almost with an edge itself sometimes—and is quite beyond the grasp of any but hands of iron. Now, the American axe feels balanced like a sword ; this is because of the peculiar curve of the handle. To strike you stand with the left foot slightly forward, and the left hand uppermost : the 'S' curve (it is of course not nearly so crooked as the letter) of the American axe adjusts itself to the anatomy of the attitude, so to speak.

The straight English handle does not ; it is stiff,

and strains the muscles; but the common 'great axe' has the advantage that it is also used for splitting logs and gnarled 'butts.' An American axe is too beautiful a tool for that rude work. The American was designed to strike at the trunk of the tree several feet from the ground, the English axe is always directed to the great roots at the base.

A dexterous woodman can swing his tool alternately left hand or right hand uppermost. The difference looks trifling; but try it, and you will be astonished at the difficulty. The blows echo and the chips fly, till the base of the tree, that naturally is much larger, is reduced to the size of the trunk or less. Now a pause, while one swarms up to 'line' it —*i.e.* to attach a rope as high as possible to guide the 'stick' in its fall.

It is commonly said that in climbing it is best to look up—a maxim that has been used for moral illustrations; but it is a mistake. In ascending a tree you should never look higher than the brim of your hat, unless when quite still and resting on a branch; temporary blindness would be the penalty in this case. Particles of decayed bark, the borings of insects in dead wood, dust, and fragments of twigs, rush down in little streams and fill the eyes. The quantity of woody powder that adheres to a tree is

surprising ; every motion dislodges it from a thousand minute crevices.   As for firs, in climbing a fir
one cannot look up at all—dead sticks, needles, and
dust pour down, and the branches are so thick together that the head has to be forced through them.
The line fixed, the saw is applied, and by slow
degrees the butt cut nearly through.   Unless much
overbalanced on one side by the limbs, an oak will
stand on a still day when almost off.

Some now seize the rope, and alternately pull and
slacken, which gives the great tree a tottering movement.   One more daring than the rest drives a wedge
into the saw-cut as it opens when the tree sways.   It
sways—it staggers ; a loud crack as the fibres part,
then with a slow heave over it goes, and, descending,
twists upon the base.   The vast limbs plough into
the sward ; the twigs are crushed ; the boughs, after
striking the earth, rebound and swish upwards.   See
that you stand clear, for the least branch will thresh
you down.   The flat surface of the exposed butt is
blue with stains from the steel of the saw.

Light taps with a small sharp axe, that cut the
rind but no deeper, ring the trunk at intervals.   Then
the barking irons are inserted ; they are rods of iron
forged at the top something like a narrow shallow
spoon.   The bark from the trunk comes off in huge

semi-cylinders almost large enough for a canoe. But that from the branches is best. You may mark how at the base the bark is two inches thick, lessening to a few lines on the topmost boughs. If it sticks a little, hammer it with the iron : it peels with a peculiar sound, and the juicy sap glistens white between. It is this that, drying in the sun, gives the barked tree its colour : in time the wood bleaches paler, and after a winter becomes grey. Inside, the bark is white streaked with brown ; presently it will be all brown. While some strip it, others collect the pieces, and with them build toy-like sheds of bark, which is the manner of stacking it.

From the peeled tree there rises a sweet odour of sap : the green mead, the green underwood and hawthorn around, are all lit up with the genial sunbeams. The beautiful wind-anemones are gone, too tender and lovely for so rude an earth ; but the wild hyacinths droop their blue bells under the wood, and the cowslips rise in the grass. The nightingale sings without ceasing ; the soft 'coo-coo' of the dove sounds hard by ; the merry cuckoo calls as he flies from elm to elm ; the wood-pigeons rise and smite their wings together over the firs. In the mere below the coots are at play ; they chase each other along the surface of the water and indulge in wild evolutions. Everything is happy. As the plough-boys stroll along they pluck the young succulent hawthorn leaves and nibble them.

It is the sweetest time of all for wandering in the wood. The brambles have not yet grown so bushy as to check the passage ; the thistles that in autumn will be as tall as the shoulder and thick as a walking-stick are as yet no bar ; burrs do not attach themselves at every step, though the broad burdock leaves are spreading wide. In its full development the burdock is almost a shrub rather than a plant, with a woody stem an inch or more in diameter.

Up in the fir trees the nests of the pigeons are sometimes so big that it appears as if they must use the same year after year, adding fresh twigs, else they could hardly attain such bulk. Those in the ash-poles are not nearly so large. In the open drives blue cartridge-cases lie among the grass, the brass part tarnished by the rain, thrown hurriedly aside from the smoking breech last autumn. But the guns are silent in the racks, though the keeper still carries his gun to shoot the vermin, which are extremely busy at this season. Vermin, however, do not quite agree among themselves : weasels and stoats are deadly enemies of mice and rats. Where rats are plentiful there they are sure to come ; they will follow a rat into a dwelling-house.

Here the green drive shows traces of the poaching it received from the thick-planted hoofs of the hunt when the leaves were off and the blast of the horn sounded fitfully as the gale carried the sound away. The vixen is now at peace, though perhaps it would scarcely be safe to wander too near the close-shaven mead where the keeper is occupied more and more every day with his pheasant-hatching. And far down on the lonely outlying farms, where even in fox-hunting England the music of the hounds is hardly heard in three years (because no great coverts cause the run to take that way), foul murder is sometimes done on Reynard or his family. A hedge-cutter marks the sleeping-place in the withies where the fox curls up by day ; and with his rusty gun, that sometimes slaughters a roaming pheasant, sends the shot through the red side of the slumbering animal. Then, thrust ignobly into a sack, he shoulders the fox and marches round from door to door, tumbling the limp body rudely down on the pitching stones to prove that the fowls will now be safe, and to be re-warded with beer and small coin. A dead fox is profit to him for a fortnight. These evil deeds of course are cloaked as far as possible.

Leaving now the wood for the lane that wanders through the meadows, a mower comes sidling up, and, looking mysteriously around with his hand behind under his coat, 'You med have un for sixpence,' he says, and produces a partridge into whose body the point of the scythe ran as she sat on her nest in the grass, and whose struggles were ended by a blow from the rubber or whetstone flung at her head. He has got the eggs somewhere hidden under a swathe.

The men that are so expert at finding partridges' eggs to sell to the keepers know well beforehand whereabouts the birds are likely to lay. If a stranger who had made no previous observations went into the fields to find these eggs, with full permission to do so, he would probably wander in vain. The grass is long, and the nest has little to distinguish it from the ground; the old bird will sit so close that one may pass almost over her. Without a right of search in open daylight the difficulty is of course much greater. A man cannot quarter the fields when the crop is high and leave no trail.

Farmers object to the trampling and damage of their property; and a keeper does not like to see a labourer loafing about, because he is not certain that the eggs when found will be conscientiously delivered to him. They may be taken elsewhere, or they may even be broken out of spite if the finder thinks he has a grudge to repay. Now that every field is enclosed, and for the most part well cultivated and looked after, the business of the egg-stealer is considerably diminished. He cannot roam over the country at his fancy ; his egg-finding is nearly restricted to the locality of which he possesses minute knowledge.

Thus workmen engaged in the towns, but sleeping several miles out in the villages, can keep a register of the slight indications they observe morning after morning as they cross the fields by the footpath to their labour. Early in the spring they notice that the partridges have paired : as time advances they see the pair day after day in the same meadow, and mark the spot. Those who work in the fields, again, have still better opportunities : the bird-keeping lads too have little else to do at that season than watch for nests. In the meadows the labourer as he walks to and fro with the ' bush ' passes over every inch of the ground. The ' bush ' is a mass of thorn bushes fixed in a frame and drawn by a horse ; it acts like a light harrow, and leaves the meadow in strips like the pile of green velvet, stroked in narrow bands, one this way, one that, laying the grass blades in the directions it travels. Solitary work of this kind—for

it requires but one man—is very favourable to observation. When the proper time arrives the searcher
knows within a little where the nest must be, and has
but a small space to beat.

The pheasant being so large a bird, its motions are
easy to watch ; and the nest is speedily found, because,
being in the hedge or under bushes, there is a definite
place in which to look, instead of the broad surface
of the field. Pheasants will get out of the preserves in
the breeding season and wander into the mounds, so
that the space the keeper has to range is then enlarged
threefold. Both pheasants and partridges are frequently killed on their nests ; when the eggs are hard
the birds remain to the last moment, and are often
knocked over.

Besides poachers, the eggs have to run the chance
of being destroyed by carrion crows, and occasionally
by rooks. Rooks, though generally cleanly feeders,
will at times eat almost anything, from a mussel to a
fledgeling bird. Magpies and jays are accused of
being equally dangerous enemies of eggs and young
birds, and so too are snakes. Weasels, stoats, and rats
spare neither egg, parents, nor offspring. Some of the
dogs that run wild will devour eggs ; and hawks
pounce on the brood if they see an opportunity. Owls
are said to do the same. The fitchew, the badger,

and the hedgehog have a similarly evil reputation; but the first is rare, the second almost exterminated in many districts; the third—the poor hedgehog—is common, and some keepers have a bitter dislike to them. Swine are credited with the same mischief as the worst of vermin at this particular season; but nowadays swine are not allowed to run wild in cultivated districts, except in the autumn when the acorns are falling.

As the nests are on the ground they are peculiarly accessible, and the eggs, being large, are tempting. Perhaps the mowing machine is as destructive as anything; and after all these there is the risk of a wet season and of disease. Let the care exercised be never so great, a certain amount of mortality must occur.

While the young partridges gradually become strong and swift, the nuts are increasing in size, and ripening upon the bough. The very word hazel has a pleasant sound—not a nut-tree hedge existed in the neighbourhood that we did not know and visit. We noted the progress of the bushes from the earliest spring, and the catkins to the perfect nut.

There are threads of brilliant scarlet upon the hazel in February, though the gloom of winter lingers and the 'Shuck—a—sheck!' of the fieldfare fleeing before the snow sounds overhead. On the slender branches grow green ovals, from whose tips tiny scarlet plumes rise and curl over.

It often happens that while the tall rods with speckled bark grow vigorously the stole is hollow and decaying when the hardy fern flourishes around it. Before the summer ricks are all carted the nuts are full of sweet milky matter, and the shell begins to harden. A hazel bough with a good crook is then sought by the men that are thinking of the wheat harvest : they trim it for a 'vagging' stick, with which to pull the straw towards them. True reaping is now never seen : 'vagging' makes the short stubble that forces the partridges into the turnips. Maple boughs, whose bark is so strongly ribbed, are also good for 'vagging' sticks.

Nut-tree is used for bonds to tie up faggots, and split for the shepherds' hurdles In winter sometimes a store of nuts and acorns may be seen fallen in a stream down the side of a bank, scratched out from a mouse's hole, as they say, by Reynard, who devours the little provident creature without regard for its wisdom. So that man and wild animals derive pleasure or use from the hazel in many ways. When the nuts are ripe the carters' lads do not care to ride sideways on the broad backs of the horses as they jog homewards along the lane, but are ever in the hedges.

There were plenty in the double-mounds to which we had access; but the shepherd, who had learned his craft on the Downs, said that the nuts grew there in such immense quantities as determined us to see them. Sitting on the felled ash under the shade of the hawthorn hedge, where the butcher-birds every year used to stick the humble-bees on the thorns, he described the route—a mere waggon track—and the situation of the largest copses.

The waggon track we found crossed the elevated plains close under and between the Downs, following at the foot, as it seemed, for an endless distance the curve of a range. The slope bounded the track on one side: on the other it was enclosed by a low bank covered with dead thorn thickly entangled, which enclosed the cornfields. The space between the hedge and the hill was as far as we could throw one of the bleached flints lying on the sward. It was dotted with hawthorn trees and furze, and full of dry brown grass. A few scattered firs, the remnants of extinct plantations, grew on the slope, and green 'fairy rings' marked it here and there.

These fairy rings have a somewhat different appearance from the dark green semicircles found in

the meadows and called by the same name : the latter
are often only segments of circles, are found near
hedges, and almost always either under a tree or
where a tree has been.   There were more mushrooms
on the side of the hill than we cared to carry.   Some
eat mushrooms raw—fresh as taken from the ground,
with a little salt : to me the taste is then too strong.
Of the many ways of cooking them the simplest is
the best ; that is, on a gridiron over wood embers on
the hearth.

Every few minutes a hare started out of the dry
grass : he always scampered up the Down and stopped
to look at us from the ridge.   The hare runs faster
up hill than down.   By the cornfields there were wire
nettings to stop them ; but nothing is easier than for
any passer-by who feels an interest in hares and rabbits,
and does not like to see them jealously excluded, to
open a gap.   Hares were very numerous—temptingly
so.   Not far from where the track crossed a lonely
road was a gipsy encampment ; that swarthy people
are ever about when anything is going on, and the
reapers were busy in the corn.   The dead dry thorns
of the hedge answered very well to boil their pot
with.   Their tents, formed by thrusting the ends of
long bent rods like half-hoops into the turf, looked
dark like the canvas of a barge.

These 'gips'—country folk do not say gipsy—
were unknown to us ; but we were on terms with some
members of a tribe who called at our house several
times in the course of the year to buy willow. The men
wore golden earrings, and bought 'Black Sally,' a
withy that has a dark bark, for pegs, and 'bolts' of
osier for basket-making. A bolt is a bundle of forty
inches in circumference. Though the women tell
fortunes, and mix the 'dark man' and the 'light
man,' the 'journey' and the 'letter' to perfection, till
the ladies half believe, I doubt if they know much
of true palmistry. The magic of the past always had
a charm for me. I had learned to know the lines,
from that which winds along at the base of the
thumb-ball and if clear means health and long life,
to that which crosses close to the fingers and
indicates the course of love, and had traced them on
many a delicate palm. So that the 'gips' could tell
me nothing new.

The women are the hardiest in the country ; they
simply ignore the weather. Even the hedgers and
ditchers and the sturdiest labourers choose the lee
side of the hedge when they pause to eat their lun-
cheons ; but the 'gips' do not trouble to seek such
shelter. Passing over the hills one winter's day,
when the Downs looked all alike, being covered with

snow, I came across a ' gip ' family sitting on the ground in a lane, old and young exposed to the blast. In that there was nothing remarkable, but I recollect it because the young mother, handsome in the style of her race, had her neck and brown bust quite bare, and the white snowflakes drove thickly aslant upon her. Their complexion looks more dusky in winter, so that the contrast of the colours made me wish for an artist to paint it. And he might have put the grey embers of a fire gone out, and the twisted stem of a hawthorn bush with red haws above.

A mile beyond the gipsy tents we entered among the copses : scattered ash plantations, and hazel thickets with narrow green tracks between. Further in the nut-tree bushes were more numerous, and we became separated though within call. Presently a low whistle like the peewit's (our signal) called me to Orion. On the border of a thicket, near an open field of swedes, he had found a hare in a wire. It was a beauty—the soft fur smooth to stroke, not so much as a shot-hole in the black-marked ears. Wired or netted hares and rabbits are much preferred by the dealers to those that have been shot—and so, too, netted partridges—because they look so clean and tempt the purchaser. The blacksmith Ikey, who bought our rabbits, used to sew up the shot wounds when they were much knocked about, and trimmed up the shattered ones in the cleverest way.

To pull up the plug and take wire and hare too was the first impulse; yet we hesitated. Why did the man who set the snare let his game lie till that hour of the day? He should have visited it long before: it had a suspicious look altogether. It would also have been nearly impossible to carry the hare so many miles by daylight and past villages: even with the largest pockets it would have been doubtful, for the hare had stiffened as he lay stretched out. So, carefully replacing him just as we found him, we left the spot and re-entered the copse.

The shepherd certainly was right; the quantity of nuts was immense: the best and largest bunches grew at the edge of the thickets, perhaps because they received more air and light than the bushes within that were surrounded by boughs. It thus happened that we were in the green pathway when some one suddenly spoke from behind, and, turning, there was a man in a velveteen jacket who had just stepped out of the bushes. The keeper was pleasant enough and readily allowed us to handle his gun—a very good weapon, though a little thin at the muzzle—for a man likes to see his gun admired. He said there were finer nuts in a valley he pointed out, and then carefully instructed us how to get back into the waggon track without returning by the same path. An old barn was the landmark ; and, with a request from him not to break the bushes, he left us.

Down in the wooded vale we paused. The whole thing was now clear : the hare in the wire was a trap laid for the ' gips,' whose camp was below. The keeper had been waiting about doubtless where he could command the various tracks up the hill, had seen us come that way, and did not wish us to return in the same direction ; because if the ' gip ' saw any one at all he would not approach his snare. Whether the hare had actually been caught by the wire, or had been put in by the keeper, it was not easy to tell.

We wandered on in the valley wood, going from bush to bush, little heeding whither we went. There are no woods so silent as the nut-tree ; there is scarce a sound in them at that time except the occasional rustle of a rabbit, and the 'thump, thump' they sometimes make underground in their buries after a sudden fright. So that the keen plaintive whistle of a kingfisher was almost startling. But we soon found the stream in the hollow. Broader than a brook and yet not quite a river, it flowed swift and clear, so that every flint at the bottom was visible. The nut-tree bushes came down to the edge : the ground was too firm for much rush or sedge; the streams that come out of the chalk are not so thickly fringed with vegetation as others.

Some little way along there was a rounded sarsen boulder not far from shore, whose brown top was so nearly on a level with the surface that at one moment the water just covered it, and the next left it exposed. By it we spied a trout; but the hill above gave 'Velvet' the command of the hollow; and it was too risky even to think of. After that the nuts were tame; there was nothing left but to turn homewards. As for trout-fishing, there is nothing so easy. Take the top joint off the rod, and put the wire on the second, which is stronger, fill the basket, and replace the fly. There were fellows who used to paddle in canoes up a certain river (not this little stream), pick out the largest trout, and shoot them with pistols, under pretence of practising at water-rats.

CHAPTER V

WOODLAND TWILIGHT : TRAITORS ON THE GIBBET

IN a hedge that joined a wood, and about a hundred yards from it, there was a pleasant hiding-place beside a pollard ash.   The bank was hollow with rabbit-buries : the summer heat had hardened the clay of the mound and caused it to crack and crumble wherever their excavations left a precipitous edge. Some way up the trunk of the tree an immense flat fungus projected, roughly resembling the protruding lip of a savage enlarged by the insertion of a piece of wood.   It formed a black ledge standing out seven or eight inches, two or three inches thick, and extending for a foot or more round the bark.   The pollard, indeed, was dead inside, and near the ground the black touch-wood showed.   Ash timber must become rarer year by year: for, being so useful, it is constantly cut down, while few new saplings are planted or encouraged to become trees.

In front a tangled mass of bramble arched over
the dry ditch ; it was possible to see some distance
down the bank, for nothing grew on the top itself,
the bushes all rising from either side—a peculiarity
of clay mounds. This narrow space was a favourite
promenade of the rabbits ; they usually came out
there for a few minutes first, looking about before
venturing forth into the meadows. Except a little
moss, scarcely any vegetation other than underwood
clothed the bare hard soil of the mound ; and for this
reason every tiny aperture that suited their purpose
was occupied by wasps.

They much prefer a clear space about the entrance
to their nests, affording an unencumbered passage :
there were two nests within a few yards of the ash.
Though so generally dreaded, wasps are really in-
offensive insects, never attacking unless previously
buffeted. You may sit close to a wasps' nest for
hours, and, if you keep still, receive no injury.
Humble-bees, too, congregate in special localities :
along one hedge half a dozen nests may be found,
while other fields are searched for them in vain.

The best time to enter such a hiding-place is a
little before the sun sinks ; for as his beams turn red
all the creatures that rest during the day begin to stir.
Then the hares start down from the uplands and

appear on the short stubble, where the level rays throw exaggerated shadows behind them. When six or eight hares are thus seen near the centre of a single field, they and their shadows seem to take possession of and occupy it.

Pheasants, though they retire to roost on the trees, often before rising come forth into the meadows adjacent to the coverts. The sward in front of the pollard ash sloped upwards gradually to the foot of a low hill planted with firs, and just outside these about half a dozen pheasants regularly appeared in the early evening. As the sun sank below the hill, and the shadow of the great beeches some distance away began to extend into the mead, they went back one by one into the firs. There they were nearly safe, for no trees give so much difficulty to the poacher. It is not easy even to shoot anything inside a fir plantation at night : as for the noose, it is almost impossible to use it. The lowest pheasant is taken first, and then the next above, like fowls perched on the rungs of a ladder ; and, indeed, it is not unlikely that those who excel in this kind of work base their operations upon previous experiences in the hen roost.

The wood pigeons begin to come home, and the wood is filled with their hollow notes : now here, now yonder, for as one ceases another takes it up. They cannot settle for some time: each as he arrives perches awhile, and then rises and tries a fresh place, so that there is a constant clattering. The green woodpecker approaches at a rapid pace—now opening, now closing his wings, and seeming to throw himself forward rather than to fly. He rushes at the trees in the hedge as though he could pierce the thick branches like a bullet. Other birds rise over or pass at the side : he goes through, arrow-like, avoiding the boughs. Instead of at once entering the wood, he stays awhile on the sward of the mead in the open.

As the pheasants generally feed in a straight line along the ground, so the lesser pied woodpecker travels across the fields from tree to tree, rarely staying on more than one branch in each, but, after examining it, leaves all that may be on other boughs and seeks another ahead. He rises round and round the dead branch in the elm, tapping it with blows that succeed each other with marvellous rapidity. He taps for the purpose of sounding the wood to see if it be hollow or bored by grubs, and to startle the insects and make them run out for his convenience. He will ascend dead branches barely half an inch thick that vibrate as he springs from them, and proceeds down the hedge towards the wood. The 'snoptop' sounds in every elm, and grows fainter as he recedes. The sound is often heard, but in the thick foliage of summer the bird escapes unseen, unless you are sitting almost under the tree when he arrives in it.

Then the rooks come drifting slowly to the beeches: they are uncertain in their hour at this season—some, indeed, scarce care to return at all; and even when quite dusk and the faint stars of summer rather show themselves than shine, twos and threes come occasionally through the gloom. A pair of doves pass swiftly, flying for the lower wood, where the ashpoles grow. The grasshoppers sing in the grass, and will continue till the dew descends. As the little bats flutter swiftly to and fro just without the hedge, the faint sound of their wings is audible as they turn : their membranes are not so silent as feathers, and they agitate them with extreme velocity. Beetles go by with a loud hum, rising from those isolated bunches of grass that may be seen in every field ; for the cows will not eat the rank green blades that grow over and hide dried dung.

A large white spot, ill-defined and shapeless in the distance and the dimness, glides along the edge of the wood, then across in front before the fir plantation, next down the hedge to the left, and presently passes within two yards, going towards the wood again along this mound. It is a white owl: he flies about five feet from the ground and absolutely without a sound. So when you are walking at night it is quite startling to have one come overhead, approaching from behind and suddenly appearing. This owl is almost fearless; unless purposely alarmed he will scarcely notice you, and not at all if you are still.

As he reaches the wood he leaves the hedge, having gone all round the field, and crosses to a small detached circular fir plantation in the centre. There he goes out of sight a minute or two; but presently appears skirting the low shed and rickyard yonder, and is finally lost behind the hedges. This round he will go every evening, and almost exactly at the same time—that is, in reference to the sun, which is the clock of nature.

Step never so quietly out from the mound, the small birds that unnoticed have come to roost in the bushes will hear it and fly off in alarm. The rabbits that are near the hedge rush in; those that are far from home crouch in the furrows and the bunches. Crossing the open field, they suddenly start as it seems from under your feet—one white tail goes dapping up and down this way, another jerks over the 'lands' that way. The moonbeams now glisten on the double-barrel ; and a bright sparkle glitters here and there as a dewdrop catches a ray.

Upon the grass a faint halo appears ; it is a narrow band of light encircling the path, an oval ring—perhaps rather horseshoe shape than oval. It glides in front, keeping ever at the same distance as you walk, as if there the eye was focussed. This is only seen when the grass is wet with dew, and better in short grass than long. Where it shines the grass looks a paler green. Passing gently along a hedge thickly timbered with oak and elm, a hawk may perhaps start forth : hawks sometimes linger by the hedges till late, but it is not often that you can shoot one at roost except in spring. Then they invariably return to roost in the nest tree, and are watched there and so shot, a gunner approaching on each side of the hedge. In the lane dark objects—rabbits—hasten away, and presently the footpath crosses the still motionless brook near where it flows into the mere.

The low brick parapet of the bridge is overgrown with mosses ; great hedges grow each side, and the willows, long uncut, almost meet in the centre. In one hedge an opening leads to a drinking-place for cattle : peering noiselessly over the parapet between the boughs, the coots and moorhens may be seen there feeding by the shore. They have come up from the mere as the ducks and teal do in the winter. The broader waters can scarcely be netted without a boat, but the brook here is the very place for a moonlight haul. The net is stretched first across the widest spot nearest to the pool, that no fish may escape. They swim up here in the daytime in shoals, perch especially ; but the night poachers are often disappointed, for the fish seem to retire to deeper waters as the darkness comes on. A black mass of mud-coated sticks, rotten twigs, and thorn bushes, entangled in the meshes, is often the only result of much toil.

Once now and then, as when a preserved pond is netted, a tremendous take occurs ; but nets are rather gone by, being so unwieldy and requiring several men to manage effectually. If they are not hung out to dry properly after being used, they soon rot. Now, a large net stretched along railings or a hedge is rather a conspicuous object, and brings suspicion on the owner. It is also so heavy after use that until wrung, which takes time, a strong man can barely carry it ; and if a sudden alarm comes it must be abandoned.

It is pleasant to rest awhile on the parapet in the shadow of the bushes. The low thud-thud of sculls in the rowlocks of a distant punt travels up the water. By-and-by a hare comes along, enters on the bridge, and almost reaches the gate in the middle before he

spies anything suspicious.   Such a spot, and, indeed,
any gateway, used to be a favourite place to set a
net, and then drive the hares towards it with a cur
dog that ran silent.   Bold must be the man that would
set a net in a footpath now, with almost every field
preserved by owner or tenant.   With a bound the
hare hies back and across the meadow : the gun comes
to the shoulder as swiftly.

On the grass lit by the moon the hare looked quite
distinct, but the moment the gaze is concentrated up.
the barrel he becomes a dim object with no defined
outline.   In shooting on the ground by twilight or in
the moonbeams, waste no time in endeavouring to
aim, but think of the hare's ears—say a couple of feet
in front of his tail—and the moment the gun feels
steady pull the trigger.   The flash and report come
together ; there is a dull indescribable sound ahead, as
some of the shot strikes home in fur and some drills
into the turf, and then a rustling in the grass.   The
moorhens dive, and the coots scuttle down the brook
towards the mere at the flash.   While yet the sul-
phurous smoke lingers, slow to disperse, over the cool
dewy sward, there comes back an echo from the wood
behind, then another from the mere, then another and
another beyond.

The distant sculls have ceased to work in the

rowlocks—those in the punt are listening to the echoes ; most likely they have been fishing for tench in the deep holes under the black shadow of the aspens. (Tench feed in the dark : if you wish to take a big one wait till it is necessary to fix a piece of white paper on the float.) Now put the empty cartridge in your pocket instead of throwing it aside ; pull the hare's neck across your knee, and hurry off. But you may safely stay to harle him ; for those very echoes that have been heard a mile round about are the best safeguard : not one man in a thousand could tell the true direction whence the sound of the explosion originated.

The pleasure of wandering in a wood was so great that it could never be resisted, and did not solely arise from the instinct of shooting. Many expeditions were made without a gun, or any implement of destruction, simply to enjoy the trees and thickets. There was one large wood very carefully preserved, and so situate in an open country as not to be easily entered. But a little observation showed that the keeper had a 'habit.' He used to come out across the wheatfields to a small wayside 'public,' and his route passed by a lonely barn and rickyard. One warm summer day I saw him come as usual to the 'public,' and while he was there quietly slipped as far as the barn and hid in it.

In July such a rickyard is very hot : heat radiates from every straw. The ground itself is dry and hard, each crevice choked with particles of white chaff; so that even the couch can hardly grow except close under the low hedge where the pink flower of the pimpernel opens to the sky. White stone staddles— short conical pillars with broad capitals—stand awaiting the load of sheaves that will shortly press on them. Every now and then a rustling in the heaps of straw indicates the presence of mice. From straw and stone and bare earth heat seems to rise up. The glare of the sunlight pours from above. The black pitched wooden walls of the barn and sheds prevent the circulation of air. There are no trees for shadow— nothing but a few elder bushes, which are crowded at intervals of a few minutes with sparrows rushing with a whirr of wings up from the standing corn.

But the high pitched roof of the barn and of the lesser sheds has a beauty of its own—the minute vegetation that has covered the tiles having changed the original dull red to an orange hue. From ridge to eaves, from end to end, it is a wide expanse of colour, only varying so much in shade as to save it from monotony. It stands out glowing, distinct against the deep blue of the sky. The 'cheep' of fledgeling sparrows comes from the crevices above;

but swallows do not frequent solitary buildings so
much as those by dwelling-houses, being especially
fond of cattle-sheds where cows are milked.

The proximity of animals apparently attracts
them : perhaps in the more exposed places there may
be dangers from birds of prey. As for the sparrows,
they are innumerable. Some are marked with white
patches—a few so much so as to make quite a show
when they fly. One handsome cock bird has a white
ring half round his neck, and his wings are a beautiful
partridge-brown. He looks larger than the common
sort ; and there are several more here that likewise
appear to exceed in size, and to have the same peculiar
brown.

After a while there came the sound of footsteps
and a low but cheerful whistle. The keeper having
slaked a thirst very natural on such a sultry day returned, and re-entered the wood. I had decided that
it would be the best plan to follow in his rear, because
then there would be little chance of crossing his course
haphazard, and the dogs would not sniff any strange
footsteps, since the footsteps would not be there till
they had gone by. To hide from the eyes of a man
is comparatively easy ; but a dog will detect an un-
wonted presence in the thickest bush, and run in and
set up a yelping, especially if it is a puppy.

It was not more than forty yards from the barn to the wood : there was no mound or hedge, but a narrow, deep, and dry watercourse, a surface drain, ran across. Stooping a little and taking off my hat, I walked in this, so that the wheat each side rose above me and gave a perfect shelter.   This precaution was necessary, because on the right there rose a steep Down, from whose summit the level wheat-fields could be easily surveyed.   So near was it that I could distinguish the tracks of the hares worn in the short grass.   But if you take off your hat no one can distinguish you in a wheat-field, more particularly if your hair is light : nor even in a hedge.

Where the drain or furrow entered the wood was a wire-netting firmly fixed, and over it tall pitched palings, sharp at the top.   The wood was enclosed with a thick hawthorn hedge that looked impassable ; but the keeper's footsteps, treading down the hedge-parsley and brushing aside the 'gicks,' guided me behind a bush where was a very convenient gap. These signs and the smooth-worn bark of an ash against which it was needful to push proved that this quiet path was used somewhat frequently.

Inside the wood the grass and the bluebell leaves —the bloom past and ripening to seed—so hung over the trail that it was difficult to follow.   It wound

about the ash stoles in the most circuitous manner—
now to avoid the thistles, now a bramble thicket, or
a hollow filled with nettles. Then the ash poles were
clothed with the glory of the woodbine—one mass of
white and yellow wax-like flowers to a height of eight
or nine feet, and forming a curtain of bloom from
branch to branch.

After awhile I became aware that the trail was
approaching the hill. At the foot it branched ; and
the question arose whether to follow the fork that zig-
zagged up among the thickets or that which seemed to
plunge into the recesses beneath. I had never been
in this wood before—the time was selected because
it was probable that the keeper would be extremely
occupied with his pheasant chicks. Though the earth
was so hard in the exposed rick-yard, here the clayey
ground was still moist under the shadow of the leaves.
Examining the path more closely, I easily distinguished
the impression of the keeper's boot: the iron toe-plate
has left an almost perfect impression, and there were
the deep grooves formed by the claws of his dog as
it had scrambled up the declivity and the pad slipped
on the clay.

As he had taken the upward path, no doubt it
led direct to the pheasants, which were sure to be on
the hill itself, or a dry and healthy slope. I therefore

took the other trail, since I must otherwise have over-
taken him ; for he would stay long among his chicks :
just as an old-fashioned farmer lingers at a gate,
gazing on his sheep. Advancing along the lower
path, after some fifteen minutes it turned sharply to
the right, and I stood under the precipitous cliff-like
edge of the hill in a narrow coombe. The earth at
the top hung over the verge, and beech-trees stood as
it seemed in the act to topple, their exposed roots
twisting to and fro before they re-entered the face of
the precipice. Large masses of chalky rubble had
actually fallen, and others were all but detached.
The coombe of course could be overlooked from
thence ; but a moment's reflection convinced me there
was no risk, for who would dare to go near enough
to the edge to look down?

The coombe was full of fir-trees ; and by them
stood a long narrow shed—the roof ruinous, but the
plank walls intact. It had originally been erected in
a field, since planted for covers. This long shed, a
greenish grey from age and mouldering wood, became
a place of much interest. Along the back there were
three rows of weasels and stoats nailed through the
head or neck to the planks. There had been a
hundred in each row—about three hundred altogether.
The lapse of time had entirely dissipated the substance

of many on the upper row ; nothing remained but the grim and rusty nail. Further along there hung small strips without shape. Beyond these the nails supported something that had a rough outline still of the animal. In the second row the dried and shrivelled creatures were closely wrapped in nature's mummy-cloth of green ; in the third, some of those last exposed still retained a dull brown colour. None were recent. Above, under the eaves, the spiders' webs had thickly gathered ; beneath, the nettles flourished.

But the end of the shed was the place where the more distinguished offenders were gibbeted. A foot-path, well worn and evidently much used, went by this end, and, as I afterwards ascertained, communicated with the mansion above and the keeper's cottage some distance below. Every passenger between must pass the gallows where the show of more noble traitors gave proof of the keeper's loyal activity. Four shorter rows rose in tiers. To the nails at the top strong beaks and black feathers adhered, much bedraggled and ruffled by weather. These crows had long been dead : the keeper when he shot a crow did not trouble to have it carried home, unless a nail was conspicuously vacant. The ignoble bird was left where he fell.

On the next row the black and white of magpies

and the blue of jays alternated.   Many of the magpies had been despoiled of their tails, and some of
their wings, the feathers being saleable.   The jays
were more numerous, and untouched ; they were slain
in such numbers that the market for their plumage
was glutted.   Though the bodies were shrunken, the
feathers were in fair condition.   Magpies' nests are so
large that in winter, when the leaves are off the trees,
they cannot but be seen, and, the spot being marked,
in the summer old and young are easily destroyed
Hawks filled the third row.   The kestrels were the
most numerous, but there were many sparrow-hawks.
These made a great show, and were stuck so closely
that a feather could hardly be thrust between them.
In the midst, quite smothered under their larger wings,
were the remains of a smaller bird—probably a
merlin.   But the last and lowest row, that was also
nearest, or on a level with the face of a person looking at the gallows, was the most striking.

This grand tier was crowded with owls—not
arranged in any order, but haphazard, causing a fine
mixture of colour.   Clearly this gallery was constantly renewed.   The white owl gave the prevalent
tint, side by side with the brown wood owls, and
scattered among the rest, a few long horned owls—a
mingling of white, yellowish brown, and tawny feathers,

Though numerous here, yet trap and gun have so reduced the wood owls that you may listen half the night by a cover and never hear the 'Who-hoo' that seems to demand your name.

The barn owls are more liable to be shot, because they are more conspicuous ; but, on the other hand, as they often breed and reside away from covers, they seem to escape. For months past one of these has sailed by my window every evening uttering a hissing 'skir-r-r.' Here, some were nailed with their backs to the wall, that they might not hide their guilty faces.

The delicate texture of the owl's feathers is very remarkable : these birds remind me of a huge moth. The owls were more showy than the hawks, though it is commonly said that without sunlight there is no colour—as in the case of plants grown in darkness. Yet the hawks are day birds, while the owls fly by night. There came the sound of footsteps ; and I retreated, casting one glance backward at the black and white, the blue and brown colours that streaked the wall, while the dull green weasels were in perpetual shadow. By night the bats would flit round and about that gloomy place. It would not do to return by the same path, lest another keeper might be coming up it ; so I stepped into the wood itself.

To those who walk only in the roads, hawks and

owls seem almost rare. But a wood is a place to which they all flock ; and any wanderer from the north or west naturally tends thither. This wood is of large extent ; but even to the smaller plantations of the Downs it is wonderful what a number come in the course of a year. Besides the shed just visited there would be certain to be another more or less ornamented near the keeper's cottage, and probably others scattered about, where the commoner vermin could be nailed without the trouble of carrying them far away. Only the owls and hawks, magpies, and such more striking evidences of slaughter were collected here, and almost daily renewed.

To get into the wood was much easier than to get out, on account of the thick hedge, palings, and high sharp-sparred gates ; but I found a dry ditch where it was possible to creep under the bushes into a meadow where was a footpath.

CHAPTER VI

LURCHER-LAND: 'THE PARK'

THE time of the apple-bloom is the most delicious season in Sarsen village. It is scarcely possible to obtain a view of the place, although it is built on the last slope of the Downs, because just where the ground drops and the eye expects an open space plantations of fir and the tops of tall poplars and elms intercept the glance. In ascending from the level meadows of the vale thick double mounds, heavily timbered with elm, hide the houses until you are actually in their midst.

Those only know a country who are acquainted with its footpaths. By the roads, indeed, the outside may be seen; but the footpaths go through the heart of the land. There are routes by which mile after mile may be travelled without leaving the sward. So you may pass from village to village; now crossing green meads, now cornfields, over

brooks, past woods, through farmyard and rick 'bar-
ken.'   But such tracks are not mapped, and a stranger
misses them altogether unless under the guidance of
an old inhabitant.

At Sarsen the dusty road enters the more modern
part of the village at once, where the broad signs
hang from the taverns at the crossways and where the
loafers steadily gaze at the new comer.   The Lower
Path, after stile and hedge and elm, and grass that
glows with golden buttercups, quietly leaves the side
of the double mounds and goes straight through the
orchards.   There are fewer flowers under the trees,
and the grass grows so long and rank that it
has already fallen aslant of its own weight.   It is
choked, too, by masses of clogweed, that springs up
profusely over the site of old foundations; so that
here ancient masonry may be hidden under the earth.
Indeed, these orchards are a survival from the days
when the monks laboured in vineyard and garden, and
mayhap even of earlier times.   When once a locality
has got into the habit of growing a certain crop it
continues to produce it for century after century; and
thus there are villages famous for apple or pear or
cherry, while the district at large is not at all given
to such culture.

The trunks of the trees succeed each other in

endless ranks, like columns that support the most beautiful roof of pink and white. Here the bloom is rosy, there white prevails : the young green is hidden under the petals that are far more numerous than leaves, or even than leaves will be. Though the path really is in shadow as the branches shut out the sun, yet it seems brighter here than in the open, as if the place were illuminated by a million tiny lamps shedding the softest lustre. The light is reflected and apparently increased by the countless flowers overhead.

The forest of bloom extends acre after acre, and only ceases where hedges divide, to commence again beyond the boundary. A wicket gate, all green with a film of vegetation over the decaying wood, opens under the very eaves of a cottage, and the path goes by the door—across a narrow meadow where deep and broad trenches, green now, show where ancient stews or fishponds existed, and then through a farmyard into a lane. Tall poplars rise on either hand, but there seem to be no houses ; they stand in fact a field's breadth back from the lane, and are approached by footpaths that every few yards necessitate a stile in the hedge.

When a low thatched farmhouse does abut upon the way, the blank white wall of the rear part faces the road, and the front door opens on precisely the other side. Hard by is a row of beehives. Though the modern hives are at once more economical and humane, they have not the old associations that cling about the straw domes topped with broken earthenware to shoot off the heavy downfall of a thunderstorm.

Everywhere the apple-bloom ; the hum of bees ; children sitting on the green beside the road, their laps full of flowers ; the song of finches ; and the low murmur of water that glides over flint and stone so shadowed by plants and grasses that the sunbeams cannot reach and glisten on it. Thus the straggling flower-strewn village stretches along beneath the hill and rises up the slope, and the swallows wheel and twitter over the gables where are their hereditary nesting-places. The lane ends on a broad dusty road, and, opposite, a quiet thatched house of the larger sort stands, endways to the street, with an open pitching before the windows. There, too, the swallows' nests are crowded under the eaves, flowers are trained against the wall, and in the garden stand the same beautiful apple-trees. But within, the lower part of the windows—-that have recess seats—are guarded by horizontal rods of iron, polished by the backs of many men. It is an inn, and the rods are.

to save the panes from the impact of an excited toper's arm.

The talk to-day, as the brown brandy, which the paler cognac has not yet superseded, is consumed and the fumes of coarse tobacco and the smell of spilt beer and the faint sickly odour of evaporating spirits overpower the flowers, is of horses. The stable lads from the training stables far up on the Downs drop in or call at the door without dismounting. Once or twice in the day a tout calls and takes his 'grub,' and scribbles a report in the little back parlour. Sporting papers, beer-stained and thumb-marked, lie on the tables; framed portraits of racers hang on the walls. Burly men, who certainly cannot ride a race, but who have horse in every feature, puff cigars and chat in jerky monosyllables that to an outsider are perfectly incomprehensible. But the glib way in which heavy sums of money are spoken of conveys the impression that they dabble in enormous wealth.

There are dogs under the tables and chairs; dogs in the window-seat; dogs panting on the stone flags of the passage, after a sharp trot behind a trap, choosing the coolest spot to loll their red tongues out; dogs outside in the road; dogs standing on hind legs, and painfully lapping the water in the horse-trough; and there is a yapping of puppies in the distance. The cushions of the sofa are strewn with dogs' hairs, and once now and then a dog leisurely hops up the stair-case.

Customers are served by the landlady, a decent body enough in her way: her son, the man of the house, is up in the 'orchut' at the rear, feeding his dogs. Where the 'orchut' ends in a paddock stands a small shed: in places the thatch on the roof has fallen through in the course of years and revealed the bare rafters. The bottom part of the door has decayed, and the long nose of a greyhound is thrust out sniffing through a hole. Dickon, the said son, is delighted to undo the padlock for a visitor who is 'square.' In an instant the long hounds leap up, half a dozen at a time, and I stagger backwards, forced by the sheer vigour of their caresses against the doorpost. Dickon cannot quell the uproarious pack: he kicks the door open, and away they scamper round and round the paddock at headlong speed.

What a joy it is to them to stretch their limbs! I forget the squalor of the kennel in watching their happy gambols. I cannot drink more than one tumbler of brown brandy and water; but Dickon overlooks that weakness, feeling that I admire his greyhounds. It is arranged that I am to see them work in the autumn.

The months pass, and in his trap with the famous trotter in the shafts we roll up the village street. Apple-bloom and golden fruit too are gone, and the houses show more now among the bare trees ; but as the rim of the ruddy November sun comes forth from the edge of a cloud there appears a buff tint everywhere in the background. When elm and ash are bare the oaks retain their leaves, and these are illumined by the autumn beams. Overtopped by tall elms and hidden by the orchards, the oaks were hardly seen in summer; now they are found to be numerous and give the prevailing hue to the place.

Dickon taps the dashboard as the mare at last tops the hill, and away she speeds along the level plateau for the Downs. Two greyhounds are with us ; two more have gone on under charge of a boy. Skirting the hills a mile or two, we presently leave the road and drive over the turf: there is no track, but Dickon knows his way. The rendezvous is a small fir plantation, the young trees in which are but shoulder-high. Below is a plain entirely surrounded by the hills, and partly green with root crops : more than one flock of sheep is down there, and two teams ploughing the stubble. Neither the ploughmen nor the shepherds take the least heed of us, except to watch for the sport. The spare couple are fastened

in the trap ; the boy jumps up and takes the reins.
Dickon puts the slip on the couple that are to run
first, and we begin to range.

Just at the foot of the hill the grass is tall and
grey ; there, too, are the dead dry stalks of many
plants that cultivation has driven from the ploughed
fields and that find a refuge at the edge. A hare
starts from the very verge and makes up the Downs.
Dickon slips the hounds, and a faint halloo comes
from the shepherds and the ploughmen. It is a
beautiful sight to see the hounds bound over the
sward ; the sinewy back bends like a bow, but a bow
that, instead of an arrow, shoots itself ; the deep
chests drink the air. Is there any moment so joyful
in life as the second when the chase begins ? As we
gaze, before we even step forward, the hare is over
the ridge and out of sight. Then we race and tear
up the slope ; then the boy in the trap flaps the reins
and away goes the mare out of sight too.

Dickon is long and rawboned, a powerful fellow,
strong of limb, and twice my build ; but he sips too
often at the brown brandy, and after the first burst
I can head him. But he knows the hills and the
route the hare will take, so that I have but to keep
pace. In five minutes as we cross a ridge we see the
game again ; the hare is circling back—she passes

under us not fifty yards away, as we stand panting on
the hill. The youngest hound gains, and runs right
over her; she doubles, the older hound picks up the
running. By a furze-bush she doubles again; but
the young one turns her—the next moment she is in
the jaws of the old dog.

Again and again the hounds are slipped, now one
couple, now the other: we pant, and can scarcely
speak with running, but the wild excitement of the
hour and the sweet pure air of the Downs supply
fresh strength. The little lad brings the mare any-
where: through the furze, among the flint-pits, jolting
over the ruts, she rattles along with sure alacrity.
There are five hares in the sack under the straw when
at last we get up and slowly drive down to the highway, reaching it some two miles from where we left it.
Dickon sends the dogs home by the boy on foot; we
drive round and return to the village by a different
route, entering it from the opposite direction.

The reason of these things is that Sarsen has no
great landlord. There are fifty small proprietors, and
not a single resident magistrate. Besides the small
farmers, there are scores of cottage owners, every one
of whom is perfectly independent. Nobody cares
for anybody. It is a republic without even the semblance of a Government. It is liberty, equality, and

swearing.   As it is just within the limit of a borough,
almost all the cottagers have votes, and are not to be
trifled with.   The proximity of horse-racing establishments adds to the general atmosphere of dissipation.
Betting, card-playing, ferret-breeding and dog-fancy-
ing, poaching and politics, are the occupations of the
populace.   A little illicit badger-baiting is varied by
a little vicar-baiting ; the mass of the inhabitants are
the reddest of Reds.   Que voulez-vous ?

The edges of some large estates come up near,
but the owners would hardly like to institute a persecu-
tion of these turbulent folk.   If they did, where would
be their influence at the next election ?   If a landlord makes himself unpopular, his own personal value
depreciates.   He is a nonentity in the committee-
room, and his help rather deprecated by the party
than desired.   The Sarsen fellows are not such fools
as to break pheasant preserves in the vale ; as they
are resident, that would not answer.   They keep outside the *sanctum sanctorum* of the pheasant coverts.
But with ferret, dog, and gun, and now and then a
partridge net along the edge of the standing barley
they excel.   So, too, with the wire ; and the broad
open Downs are their happy hunting grounds, especially in misty weather.

This is the village of the apple-bloom, the loveliest

spot imaginable. After all, they are not such desperately bad fellows if you deduct their sins against the game laws. They are a jovial lot, and free with their money; they stand by one another—a great virtue in these cold-blooded days. If one gets in trouble with the law the rest subscribe the fine. They are full of knowledge of a certain sort, and you may learn anything, from the best way to hang a dog upwards.

When we reach the inn, and Dickon calls for the brown brandy, there in the bar sits a gamekeeper, whose rubicund countenance beams with good humour. He is never called upon to pay his score. Good fellow! in addition he is popular, and every one asks him to drink: besides which, a tip for a race now and then makes this world wear a smiling aspect to him.

Dickon's 'unconscious education'—absorbed rather than learnt in boyhood—had not been acquired under conditions likely to lead him to admire scenery. But, rough as he was, he was a good-natured fellow, and it was through him that I became acquainted with a very beautiful place.

The footpath to The Park went for about half a mile under the shadow of elm trees, and in spring time there was a continual noise of young rooks in the nests above. Occasionally dead twigs, either dislodged from the nests or broken off by the motions of the old birds, came rustling down. One or two nests that had been blown out strewed the sward with half a bushel of dead sticks. After the rookery the path passed a lonely dairy, where the polished brazen vessels in the skilling glittered like gold in the sunshine. Farther on came wide open meadows with numerous oak-trees scattered in the midst—the outposts of the great wood at hand. The elms were flourishing and vigorous ; but these detached oaks were decaying, and some dead, their hoar antiquity contrasting with the green grass and flowers of the mead.

The mansion was hidden by elm and chestnut, pines and sombre cedars. From the edge of the lawn the steep slope of the down rose, planted with all manner of shrubs, the walks through which were inches deep in dead leaves, needles, and fir-cones. Long neglect had permitted these to accumulate, and the yew hedges had almost grown together and covered the walk they bordered.

The woods and preserves extended along the downs, between the hills and the meadows beneath. There was one path through these woods that led into a narrow steep-sided coombe, one side of which was planted with firs. On the other was a little grass, but so thin as scarcely to cover the chalk. This side jutted out from the general line of the hills, and formed a bold bluff, whose white precipitous cliff was a landmark for many miles. In climbing the coombe, it was sometimes necessary to grasp the bunches of grass ; for it would have been impossible to recover from a slip till, bruised and shaken, you rolled to the bottom, and perhaps into the little streamlet flowing through the hollow.

The summit was of small extent, but the view beautiful. A low fence of withy had long since decayed, nothing but a few rotten stakes remaining at the very verge of the precipice. Steep as it was, there were some ledges that the rabbits frequented, making their homes in mid-air. Further along, the slope, a little less perpendicular, was covered with nut-tree bushes, where you could scramble down by holding to the boughs. There was a tradition of a foxhunter, in the excitement of the chase, forcing his horse to descend through these bushes and actually reaching the level meadows below in safety.

Impossible as it seemed, yet when the hounds were in full cry beneath it was easy to understand that in the eagerness of the moment a horseman at the top might feel tempted to join the stirring scene at any risk : for the fox frequently ran just below, making along the line of coverts ; and from that narrow perch on the cliff the whole field came into sight at once. There was Reynard slipping ahead, and two or more fields behind the foremost of the pack, while the rest, rushing after, made the hills resound with their chiding. The leaders taking the hedges, the main squadron splashing through a marshy place, the outsiders straining to come up, and the last man behind, who rode harder than any—all could be seen at the same time.

It was a lovely spot, too, for dreaming on a summer's day, reclining on the turf, with the harebells swinging in the faint breeze. The extreme solitude was its charm : no lanes or tracks other than those purely pastoral came near. There were woods on either hand ; in the fir plantations the jays chattered unceasingly. The broad landscape stretched out to the illimitable distance, till the power of the eye failed and could trace it no farther. But if the gaze was lifted it looked into blue space—the azure heaven not only overhead, but, as it seemed, all around.

Dickon was always to and fro the mansion here, and took me with him. His object was ostensibly business : now it was a horse to buy, now a fat bullock or sheep ; now it was an acre or two of wood that was to be cut. The people of the mansion were

so much from home that their existence was almost
forgotten, and they were spoken of vaguely as ‘ on the
Continent.’ There was, in fact, a lack of ready-money,
perhaps from the accumulation of settlements, that
reduced the nominal income of the head to a tithe of
what it should have been.

Yet they were too proud to have in the modern
builder, the modern upholsterer, and, most dreadful
of all, the modern ‘ gardener,’ to put in French sashes,
gilding and mirrors, and to root up the fine old yew
hedges and level the grand old trees. Such is the
usual preparation before an advertisement appears
that a mansion of ‘ historic association,’ and ‘ replete
with every modern convenience,’ is to let, with some
thousand of acres of shooting, &c.

They still kept up an establishment of servants—
after a fashion—who did much as they pleased.
Dickon was a great favourite. As for myself, a mere
dreamy lad, I could go into the woods and wander as
I liked, which was sufficient. But I recollect the
immense kitchen very well, and the polished relics of
the ancient turnspit machinery. There was a door
from it opening on a square stone-flagged court with
a vertical sun-dial on the wall ; and beyond that
ranges of disused coach-houses—all cloudy, as it were,
with cobwebs hanging on old-fashioned post-chaises.

Dickon was in love with one of the maids, a remarkably handsome girl.

She showed me the famous mantelpiece, a vast carved work, under which you could stand upright. The legend was that once a year on a certain night a sable horse and cloaked horseman rode across that great apartment, flames snorting from the horse's nostrils, and into the fireplace, disappearing with a clap of thunder. She brought me, too, an owl from the coachhouses, holding the bird by the legs firmly, her hand defended by her apron from the claws.

The butler was a little merry fellow, extremely fond of a gun, and expert in using it. He seemed to have nothing to do but tell tales and sing, except at the rare intervals when some of the family returned unexpectedly. The keeper was always up there in the kitchen ; he was as pleasant and jovial as a man could well be, though full of oaths on occasion. He was a man of one tale—of a somewhat enigmatical character. He would ask a stranger if they had ever heard of such-and-such a village where water set fire to a barn, ducks were drowned, and pigs cut their own throats, all in a single day.

It seemed that some lime had been stored in the barn, when the brook rose and flooded the place ; this slaked the lime and fired the straw, and so the barn.

Something of the same kind happens occasionally on the river barges. The ducks were in a coop fastened down, so that they could not swim on the surface of the flood, which passed over and drowned them. The pigs were floated out of the sty, and in swimming their sharp-edged hoofs struck their fat jowls just behind the ear at every stroke till they cut into the artery, and so bled to death. Where he got this history from I do not know.

One bright October morning (towards the end of the month) Dickon drove me over to the old place with his fast trotter—our double-barrels hidden under some sacks in the trap. The keeper was already waiting in the kitchen, sipping a glass of hot purl ; the butler was filling every pocket with cartridges. After some comparison of their betting-books, for Dickon, on account of his acquaintance with the training establishments, was up to most moves, we started. The keeper had to send a certain number of pheasants and other game to the absent family and their friends every now and then, and this duty was his pretext. There was plenty of shooting to be got elsewhere, but the spice of naughtiness about this was alluring.   To reach that part of the wood where it was proposed to shoot the shortest way led across some arable fields.

Fieldfares and redwings rose out of the hedges and

flew away in their peculiarly scattered manner—their flocks, though proceeding in the same direction, seeming all loose and disordered. Where the ploughs had been at work already the deep furrows were full of elm leaves, wafted as they fell from the trees in such quantities as to make the groove left by the share level with the ridges. A flock of lapwings were on the clods in an adjacent field, near enough to be seen, but far beyond gunshot. There might perhaps have been fifty birds, all facing one way and all perfectly motionless. They were, in fact, watching us intently, although not apparently looking towards us : they act so much in concert as to seem drilled. So soon as the possibility of danger had gone by each would begin to feed, moving ahead.

The path then passed through the little meadows that joined the wood : and the sunlight glistened on the dew, or rather on the hoar frost that had melted and clung in heavy drops to the grass. Here one flashed emerald ; there ruby ; another a pure brilliance like a diamond. Under foot by the stiles the fallen acorns crunched as they split into halves beneath the sudden pressure.

The leaves still left on the sycamores were marked with large black spots : the horse-chestnuts were quite bare ; and already the tips of the branches carried the

varnish-coloured sheaths of the buds that were to
appear the following spring. These stuck to the
finger if touched, as if they really had been varnished.
Through the long months of winter they would remain, till under April showers and sunshine the sheath
fell back and the green leaflets pushed up, the two
forming together a rude cross for a short time.

The day was perfectly still, and the colours of the
leaves still left glowed in the sunbeams. Beneath, the
dank bronzed fern that must soon shrivel was wet,
and hung with spiders' webs that like a slender netting
upheld the dew. The keeper swore a good deal about
a certain gentleman farmer whose lands adjoined
the estate, but who held under a different proprietor.
Between these two there was a constant bickering—
the tenant angry about the damage done to his crops
by the hares and rabbits, and the keeper bitterly
resenting the tenant's watch on his movements, and
warnings to his employer that all was not quite as it
should be.

The tenant had the right to shoot, and he was
always about in the turnips—a terrible thorn in the
side of Dickon's friend. The tenant roundly declared
the keeper a rascal, and told his master so in written
communications. The keeper declared the tenant set
gins by the wood, in which the pheasants stepped and

had their legs smashed.   Then the tenant charged the keeper with trespassing ; the other retorted that he decoyed the pheasants by leaving peas till they dropped out of the pods.   In short, their hatred was always showing itself in some act of guerrilla warfare. As we approached the part of the woods fixed on, two of the keeper's assistants, carrying thick sticks, stepped from behind a hedge, and reported that they had kept a good watch, and the old fox (the tenant) had not been seen that morning.   So these fellows went round to beat, and the guns were got ready.

Sometimes you could hear the pheasants running before they reached the low-cropped hawthorn hedge at the side of the plantation ; sometimes they came so quietly as to appear suddenly out from the ditch, having crept through.   Others came with a tremendous rush through the painted leaves, rising just before the hedge ; and now and then one flew screaming high over the tops of the firs and ash-poles, his glossy neck glowing in the sunlight and his long tail floating behind.   These last pleased me most, for when the shot struck the great bird going at that rate even death could not at once arrest his progress.   The impetus carried him yards, gradually slanting downwards till he rolled in the green rush bunches.

Then a hare slipped out and ran the gauntlet, and

filled the hollow with his cries when the shot broke
his hindquarters, till the dog had him. Jays came in
couples, and green woodpeckers singly : the magpies
cunningly flew aside instead of straight ahead ; they
never could do anything straightforward. A stoat
peeped out, but went back directly when a rabbit
whose retreat had been cut off bolted over his most
insidious enemy. Every now and then Dickon's
shot when he fired high cut the twigs out of the ash
by me. Then came the distant noise of the beaters'
sticks, and the pheasants, at last thoroughly disturbed,
flew out in twos and threes at a time. Now the firing
grew fierce, and the roll of the volleys ceaseless. It
was impossible to jam the cartridges fast enough in
the breech.

A subtle flavour of sulphur filled the mouth, and
the lips became dry. Sunshine and gleaming leaves
and sky and grass seemed to all disappear in the fever
of the moment. The gun burned the hands, all
blackened by the powder ; the metal got hotter and
hotter ; the sward was poached and trampled and
dotted with cases ; shot hissed through the air and
pattered in showers on the opposite plantation ; the
eyes, bleared and bloodshot with the smoke, could
scarce see to point the tube. Pheasants fell, and no
one heeded ; pheasants escaped, and none noticed

it ; pheasants were but just winged and ran wounded
into the distant hedges ; pheasants were blown out of
all living shape and could hardly be gathered up.
Not a word spoken : a breathless haste to load and
blaze ; a storm of shot and smoke and slaughter.

CHAPTER VII

OBY AND HIS SYSTEM : THE MOUCHER'S CALENDAR

ONE dark night, as I was walking on a lonely road, I kicked against something, and but just saved myself from a fall. It was an intoxicated man lying at full length. As a rule, it is best to let such people alone ; but it occurred to me that the mail-cart was due ; with two horses harnessed tandem-fashion, and travelling at full speed, the mail would probably go over him. So I seized the fellow by the collar and dragged him out of the way. Then he sat up, and asked in a very threatening tone who I was. I mentioned my name : he grunted, and fell back on the turf, where I left him.

The incident passed out of my mind, when one afternoon a labourer called, asking for me in a mysterious manner, and refusing to communicate his business to any one else. When admitted, he pro-

duced a couple of cock pheasants from under his coat,
the tail feathers much crumpled, but otherwise in fine
condition.   These he placed on the table, remarking,
'I ain't forgot as you drawed I out of the raud thuck
night.'   I made him understand that such presents
were too embarrassing ; but he seemed anxious to do
'summat,' so I asked him to find me a few ferns and
rare plants.

This he did from time to time ; and thus a species
of acquaintanceship grew up, and I learned all about
him.   He was always called ' Oby ' (*i.e.* Obadiah), and
was the most determined poacher of a neighbouring
district—a notorious fighting man—hardened against
shame, an Ishmaelite openly contemning authority and
yet not insensible to kindness.   I give his history in
his own language—softening only the pronunciation,
that would otherwise be unintelligible.

'I lives with my granny in Thorney-lane : it be
outside the village.   My mother be married agen, you
see, to the smith : her have got a cottage as belongs
to her.   My brother have got a van and travels the
country ; and sometimes I and my wife goes with
him.   I larned to set up a wire when I went to plough
when I were a boy, but never took to it regular till
I went a-navigating [navvying] and seed what a spree
it were.

'There ain't no such chaps for poaching as they navigators in all England : I means where there be a railway a-making. I've knowed forty of 'em go out together on a Sunday, and every man had a dog, and some two ; and good dogs too—lots of 'em as you wouldn't buy for ten quid. They used to spread out like, and sweep the fields as clean as the crownd of your hat. Keepers weren't no good at all, and besides they never knowed which place us was going to make for. One of the chaps gave I a puppy, and he growed into the finest greyhound as you'd find in a day's walk. The first time I was took up before the bench I had to go to gaol, because the contractor had broke and the works was stopped, so that my mates hadn't no money to pay the fine.

'The dog was took away home to granny by my butty [comrade], but one of the gentlemen as seed it in the court sent his groom over and got it off the old woman for five pound. She thought if I hadn't the hound I should give it up, and she come and paid me out of gaol. It was a wonder as I didn't break her neck ; only her was a good woman, you see, to I. But I wouldn't have parted with that hound for a quart-full of sovereigns. Many's a time I've seed his name—they changed his name, of course—in the papers for winning coursing matches. But we let that gent as bought him have it warm : we harried his pheasants and killed the most of 'em.

'After that I came home, and took to it regular. It ain't no use unless you do it regular. If a man goes out into the fields now and then chance-like he don't get much, and is most sure to be caught—very likely in the place of somebody else the keepers were waiting for and as didn't come. I goes to work every day the same as the rest, only I always take piece-work, which I can come to when I fancy, and stay as late in the evening as suits me with a good excuse. As I knows navigating, I do a main bit of draining and water-furrowing, and I gets good wages all the year round, and never wants for a job. You see, I knows more than the fellows as have never been at nothing but plough.

'The reason I gets on so well poaching is because I'm always at work out in the fields, except when I goes with the van. I watches everything as goes on, and marks the hare's tracks and the rabbit buries, and the double mounds and little copses as the pheasants wanders off to in the autumn. I keeps a 'nation good look-out after the keeper and his men, and sees their dodges—which way they walks, and how they comes back sudden and unexpected on purpose. There's mostly one about with his eyes on me—when they sees me working on a farm they puts a man special to look after me. I never does nothing close round where I'm at work, so he waits about a main bit for nothing.

'You see by going out piece-work I visits every farm in the parish. The other men they works for one farmer for two or three or maybe twenty years; but I goes very nigh all round the place—a fortnight here and a week there, and then a month somewhere else. So I knows every hare in the parish, and all his runs and all the double mounds and copses, and the little covers in the corners of the fields. When I be at work on one place I sets my wires about half a mile away on a farm as I ain't been working on for a month, and where the keeper don't keep no special look-out now I be gone. As I goes all round, I knows the ways of all the farmers, and them as bides out late at night at their friends', and they as goes to bed early; and so I knows what paths to follow and what fields I can walk about in and never meet nobody.

'The dodge is to be always in the fields and to know everybody's ways. Then you may do just as you be a-mind. All of 'em knows I be a-poaching; but that don't make no difference for work; I can use my tools, and do it as well as any man in the country, and they be glad to get me on for 'em.

They farmers as have got their shooting be sharper than the keepers, and you can't do much there ; but they as haven't got the shooting don't take no notice. They sees my wires in the grass, and just looks the other way.   If they sees I with a gun I puts un in the ditch till they be gone by, and they don't look among the nettles.

'Some of them as got land by the wood would like I to be there all day and night.   You see, their clover and corn feeds the hares and pheasants ; and then some day when they goes into the market and passes the poultry-shop there be four or five score pheasants a-hanging up with their long tails a-sweeping in the faces of them as fed 'em.   The same with the hares and the rabbits ; and so they'd just as soon as I had 'em—and a dalled deal sooner—out of spite.   Lord bless you ! if I was to walk through their courtyards at night with a sack over my shoulders full of you knows what, and met one of 'em, he'd tell his dog to stop that yowling, and go in doors rather than see me. As for the rabbits, they hates they worse than poison. They knocks a hare over now and then themselves on the quiet—bless you ! I could tell tales on a main few, but I bean't such a fellow as that.

'But, you see I don't run no risk except from the keeper hisself, the men as helps un, and two or three

lickspittles as be always messing round after a ferreting job or some wood-cutting, and the Christmas
charities. It be enough to make a man sick to see
they. This yer parish be a very big un, and a be
preserved very high, and I can do three times as much
in he as in the next one, as ain't much preserved. So
I sticks to this un.

'Of course they tried to drive I out of un, and
wanted the cottage ; but granny had all the receipts
for the quit-rent, and my lard and all the lawyers
couldn't shove us out, and there we means to bide.
You have seed that row of oaks as grows in the hedge
behind our house. One of 'em leaned over the roof,
and one of the limbs was like to fall ; but they
wouldn't cut him, just to spite us, and the rain drip-
ping spoilt the thatch. So I just had another chimney
built at that end for an oven, and kept up the smoke
till all the tree that side died. I've had more than
one pheasant through them oaks, as draws 'em : I had
one in a gin as I put in the ditch by my garden.

' They started a tale as 'twas I as stole the lambs a
year or two ago, and they had me up for it ; but they
couldn't prove nothing agen me. Then they had
me for unhinging the gates and drowning 'em in the
water, but when they was going to try the case they
two young farmers as you know of come and said as

they did it when they was tight, and so I got off. They said as 'twas I that put the poison for the hounds when three on 'em took it and died while the hunt was on.   It were the dalledest lie!   I wouldn't hurt a dog not for nothing. The keeper hisself put that poison, I knows, 'cause he couldn't bear the pack coming to upset the pheasants. Yes, they been down upon I a main bit, but I means to bide.   All the farmers knows as I never touched no lamb, nor even pulled a turmot, and they never couldn't get no witnesses.

'After a bit I catched the keeper hisself and the policeman at it ; and there be another as knows it, and who do you think that be?   It be the man in town as got the licence to sell game as haves most of my hares: the keeper selled he a lot as the money never got to my lard's pocket and the steward never knowed of.   Look at that now!   So now he shuts his eye and axes me to drink, and give me the ferreting job in Longlands Mound ; but, Lord bless 'ee, I bean't so soft as he thinks for.

'They used to try and get me to fight the keeper when they did catch me with a wire, but I knowed as hitting is transporting, and just put my hands in my pockets and let 'em do as they liked. *They* knows I bean't afraid of 'em in the road ; I've threshed more than one of 'em, but I ain't going to jump into *that* trap. I've been before the bench, at one place and t'other, heaps of times, and paid the fine for trespass. Last time the chairman said to I, "So you be here again, Oby; we hear a good deal about you." I says, "Yes, my lard, I be here agen, but people never don't hear nothing about *you.*' That shut the old duffer up. Nobody never heard nothing of he, except at rent-audit.

'However, they all knows me now—my lard and the steward, and the keeper and the bailies, and the farmers; and they don't take half the notice of I as they used to. The keeper he don't dare, nor the policeman as I telled you, and the rest be got used to me and my ways. And I does very well one week with t'other. One week I don't take nothing, and the next I haves a good haul, chiefly hares and rabbits; 'cause of course I never goes into the wood, nor the plantations. It wants eight or ten with crape masks on for that job.

'I sets up about four wires, sometimes only two: if you haves so many it is a job to look after 'em. I stops the hare's other runs, so that she is sure to come along mine where I've got the turnpike up: the trick is to rub your hand along the runs as you want to stop, or spit on 'em, or summat like that; for a hare won't pass nothing of that sort. So pussy goes back and comes by the run as I've chose: if she comes

quick she don't holler ; if she comes slow she squeals
a bit sometimes before the wire hangs her.   Very
often I bean't fur off and stops the squealing.   That's
why I can't use a gin—it makes 'em holler so.   I
ferrets a goodish few rabbits on bright nights in winter.

'As for the pheasants, I gets them mostly about
acorn-time ; they comes out of the plantations then.
I keeps clear of the plantations, because, besides the
men a-watching, they have got dogs chained up, and
alarm-guns as goes off if you steps on the spring ;
and some have got a string stretched along as you
be pretty sure to kick against, and then, bang ! and
all the dogs sets up a yowling.   Of course it's only
powder, but it brings the keepers along.   But when
the acorns and the berries be ripe, the pheasants
comes out along the hedges after 'em, and gets up at
the haws and such like.   They wanders for miles, and
as they don't care to go all the way back to roost
they bides in the little copses as I told you of.   They
come to the same copses every year, which is curious,
as most of them as will come this year will be shot
before next.

'If I can't get 'em the fust night, I just throws a
handful or two of peas about the place, and they'll
be sure to stay, and likely enough bring two or three
more.   I mostly shoots 'em with just a little puff of

powder as you wouldn't hear across one field, especially
if it's a windy night. I had a air-gun, as was took
from me, but he weren't much go : I likes a gun as
throws the shot wide, but I never shoots any but
roosters, unless I catch 'em standing still.

'All as I can tell you is as the dodge is this : you
watch everybody, and be always in the fields, and
always work one parish till you knows every hare in
un, and always work by yourself and don't have no
mates.'

There were several other curious characters whom
we frequently saw at work. The mouchers were
about all the year round, and seemed to live in, or
by the hedges, as much as the mice. These men
probably see more than the most careful observer,
without giving it a thought.

In January the ice that freezes in the ditches
appears of a dark colour, because it lies without intervening water on the dead brown leaves. Their tint
shows through the translucent crystal, but near the
edge of the ice three white lines or bands run round.
If by any chance the ice gets broken or upturned,
these white bands are seen to be caused by flanges
projecting from the under surface, almost like stands.
They are sometimes connected in such a way that
the parallel flanges appear like the letter 'h' with the

two down-strokes much prolonged. In the morning
the chalky rubble brought from the pits upon the
Downs and used for mending gateways leading into
the fields glistens brightly. Upon the surface of each
piece of rubble there adheres a thin coating of ice:
if this be lightly struck it falls off, and with it a flake
of the chalk. As it melts, too, the chalk splits and
crumbles; and thus in an ordinary gateway the
same process may be seen that disintegrates the most
majestic cliff.

The stubbles—those that still remain—are full of
linnets, upon which the mouching fowler preys in the
late autumn. And when at the end of January the
occasional sunbeams give some faint hope of spring,
he wanders through the lanes carrying a decoy bird
in a darkened cage, and a few boughs of privet studded
with black berries and bound round with rushes for
the convenience of handling.

The female yellow-hammers, whose hues are not so
brilliant as those of the male birds, seem as winter
approaches to flock together, and roam the hedges
and stubble fields in bevies. Where loads of corn
have passed through gates the bushes often catch
some straws, and the tops of the gateposts, being
decayed and ragged, hold others. These are neglected
while the seeds among the stubble, the charlock, and

the autumn dandelion are plentiful and while the ears left by the gleaners may still be found. But in the shadowless winter days, hard and cold, each scattered straw is sought for.

A few days before the new year [1879] opened I saw a yellow-hammer attacking, in a very ingenious manner, a straw that hung pendent, the ear downwards, from the post of a windy gateway. She fluttered up from the ground, clung to the ear, and outspread her wings, keeping them rigid. The draught acted on the wings, just as the breeze does on a paper kite, and there the bird remained supported without an effort while the ear was picked. Now and then the balance was lost, but she was soon up again, and again used the wind to maintain her position. The brilliant cockbirds return in the early spring, or at least appear to do so, for the habits of birds are sometimes quite local.

It is probable that in severe and continued frost many hedgehogs die. On January 19 [1879], in the midst of the sharp weather, a hedgehog came to the door opening on the garden at night, and was taken in. Though carefully tended, the poor creature died next day : it was so weak it could scarcely roll itself into a ball. As the vital heat declined the fleas deserted their host and issued from among the spines.

In February, unless it be a mild season, the mounds are still bare; and then under the bushes the ground may be sometimes seen strewn with bulbous roots, apparently of the blue-bell, lying thickly together and entirely exposed.

The moucher now carries a bill-hook, and as he shambles along the road keeps a sharp look-out for briars. When he sees one the roots of which are not difficult to get at, and whose tall upright stem is green—if dark it is too old—he hacks it off with as much of the root as possible. The lesser branches are cut, and the stem generally trimmed; it is then sold to the gardeners as the stock on which to graft standard roses. In a few hours as he travels he will get together quite a bundle of such briars. He also collects moss, which is sold for the purpose of placing in flowerpots to hide the earth. The moss preferred is that growing on and round stoles.

The melting of the snow and the rains in February cause the ditches to overflow and form shallow pools in the level meadows. Into these sometimes the rooks wade as far as the length of their legs allows them, till the discoloured yellow water almost touches the lower part of the breast. The moucher searches for small shell snails, of which quantities are sold as food for cage birds, and cuts small 'turfs' a few inches square from the green by the roadside. These are in great request for larks, especially at this time of the year, when they begin to sing with all their might.

Large flocks of woodpigeons are now in every field where the tender swede and turnip tops are sprouting green and succulent. These 'tops' are the moucher's first great crop of the year. The time that they appear varies with the weather : in a mild winter some may be found early in January ; if the frost has been severe there may be none till March. These the moucher gathers by stealth ; he speedily fills a sack, and goes off with it to the nearest town. Turnip-tops are much more in demand now than formerly, and the stealing of them a more serious matter. This trade lasts some time, till the tops become too large and garden greens take their place.

In going to and fro the fields the moucher searches the banks and digs out primrose 'mars,' and ferns with the root attached, which he hawks from door to door in the town. He also gathers quantities of spring flowers, as violets. This spring [1879], owing to the severity of the season, there were practically none to gather, and when the weather moderated the garden flowers preceded those of the

hedge. Till the 10th of March not a spot of colour
was to be seen. About that time bright yellow
flowers appeared suddenly on the clayey banks and
waste places, and among the hard clay lumps of
fields ploughed but not sown.

The brilliant yellow formed a striking contrast
to the dull brown of the clods, there being no
green leaf to moderate the extremes of tint. These
were the blossoms of the coltsfoot, that sends up a
stalk surrounded with faintly rosy scales. Several
such stalks often spring from a single clod : lift the
heavy clod, and you have half a dozen flowers, a
whole bunch, without a single leaf. Usually the
young grasses and the seed-leaves of plants have
risen up and supply a general green ; but this year
the coltsfoot bloomed unsupported, studding the dark
ground with gold.

Now the frogs are busy, and the land lizards come
forth. Even these the moucher sometimes captures ;
for there is nothing so strange but that some one
selects it for a pet. The mad March hares scamper
about in broad daylight over the corn, whose pale
green blades rise in straight lines a few inches above
the soil. They are chasing their skittish loves, instead of soberly dreaming the day away in a bunch
of grass. The ploughman walks in the furrow his

share has made, and presently stops to measure the 'lands' with the spud. His horses halt dead in the tenth of a second at the sound of his voice, glad to rest for a minute from their toil. Work there is in plenty now, for stone-picking, hoeing, and other matters must be attended to ; but the moucher lounges in the road decoying chaffinches, or perhaps earns a shilling by driving some dealer's cattle home from fair and market.

By April his second great crop is ready—the watercress ; the precise time of course varies very much, and at first the quantities are small. The hedges are now fast putting on the robe of green that gradually hides the wreck of last year's growth. The withered head of the teazle, black from the rain, falls and disappears. Great burdock stems lie prostrate. Thick and hard as they are while the sap is still in them, in winter the wet ground rots the lower part till the blast overthrows the stalk. The hollow 'gicks' too, that lately stood almost to the shoulder, is down, or slanting, temporarily supported by some branch. Just between the root and the stalk it has decayed till nothing but a narrow strip connects the dry upper part with the earth. The moucher sells the nests and eggs of small birds to townsfolk who cannot themselves wander among the fields, but who love to see something that reminds them of the green meadows.

As the season advances and the summer comes he gathers vast quantities of dandelion leaves, parsley, sowthistle, clover, and so forth, as food for the tame rabbits kept in towns. If his haunt be not far from a river, he spends hours collecting bait—worm and grub and fly—for the boatmen, who sell them again to the anglers.

Again there is work in the meadows—the hay-making is about, and the farmers are anxious for men. But the moucher passes by and looks for quaking grass, bunches of which have a ready sale. Fledgeling goldfinches and linnets, young rabbits, young squirrels, even the nest of the harvest-trow mouse, and occasionally a snake, bring him in a little money. He picks the forget-me-nots from the streams and the 'blue-bottle' from the corn : bunches of the latter are sometimes sold in London at a price that seems extravagant to those who have seen whole fields tinted with its beautiful azure. By-and-by the golden wheat calls for an army of workers ; but the moucher passes on and gathers groundsel.

Then come the mushrooms : he knows the best places, and soon fills a basket full of ' buttons,' picking them very early in the morning. These are then put in 'punnets' by the greengrocers and retailed at a high price. Later the blackberries ripen and form his third great crop; the quantity he brings in to the towns is astonishing, and still there is always a customer. The blackberry harvest lasts for several weeks, as the berries do not all ripen at once, but successively, and is supplemented by elderberries and sloes. The moucher sometimes sleeps on the heaps of disused tan in a tanyard : tanyards are generally on the banks of small rivers. The tan is said to possess the property of preserving those who sleep on it from chills and cold, though they may lie quite exposed to the weather.

There is generally at least one such a man as this about the outskirts of market towns, and he is an 'original' best defined by negatives. He is not a tramp, for he never enters the casual wards and never begs—that is, of strangers ; though there are certain farmhouses where he calls once now and then and gets a slice of bread and cheese and a pint of ale. He brings to the farmhouse a duck's egg that has been dropped in the brook by some negligent bird, or carries intelligence of the nest made by some roaming goose in a distant withy-bed. Or once, perhaps, he found a sheep on its back in a narrow furrow, unable to get up and likely to die if not assisted, and by helping the animal to gain its legs earned a title to the owner's gratitude.

He is not a thief; apples and plums and so on are quite safe, though the turnip-tops are not : there is a subtle casuistry involved here—the distinction between the quasi-wild and the garden product.   He is not a poacher in the sense of entering coverts, or even snaring a rabbit.   If the pheasants are so numerous and so tame that passing carters have to whip them out of the way of the horses, it is hardly wonderful if one should disappear now and then.   Nor is he like the Running Jack that used to accompany the more famous packs of foxhounds, opening gates, holding horses, and a hundred other little services, and who kept up with the hunt by sheer fleetness of foot.

Yet he is fleet of foot in his way, though never seen to run ; he *pads* along on naked feet like an animal, never straightening the leg, but always keeping the knee a little bent.   With a basket of watercress slung at his back by a piece of tar-cord, he travels rapidly in this way ; his feet go 'pad, pad,' on the thick white dust, and he easily overtakes a good walker and keeps up the pace for miles without exertion.   The watercress is a great staple, because it lasts for so many months.   Seeing the nimble way in which he gathers it, thrusting aside the brook-lime, breaking off the coarser sprays, snipping away pieces of root, sorting and washing, and thinking of the amount of work to be got through before a shilling is earned, one would imagine that the slow, idling life of the labourer, with his regular wages, would be far more enticing.

Near the stream the ground is perhaps peaty: little black pools appear between tufts of grass, some of them streaked with a reddish or yellowish slime that glistens on the surface of the dark water ; and as you step there is a hissing sound as the spongy earth yields, and a tiny spout is forced forth several yards distant. Some of the drier part of the soil the moucher takes to sell for use in gardens and flower-pots as peat.

The years roll on, and he grows old. But no feebleness of body or mind can induce him to enter the workhouse : he cannot quit his old haunts. Let it rain or sleet, or let the furious gale drive broken boughs across the road, he still sleeps in some shed or under a straw-rick. In sheer pity he is committed every now and then to prison for vagabondage—not for punishment, but in order to save him from himself. It is in vain ; the moment he is out he returns to his habits. All he wants is a little beer— he is not a drunkard—and a little tobacco, and the hedges. Some chilly evening, as the shadows thicken, he shambles out of the town, and seeks the limekiln in the ploughed field, where, the substratum being limestone, the farmer burns it. Near the top of the kiln the ground is warm ; there he reclines and sleeps.

The night goes on. Out from the broken blocks of stone now and again there rises a lambent flame, to shine like a meteor for a moment and then disappear. The rain falls. The moucher moves uneasily in his sleep ; instinctively he rolls or crawls towards the warmth, and presently lies extended on the top of the kiln. The wings of the water-fowl hurtle in the air as they go over ; by-and-by the heron utters his loud call.

Very early in the morning the quarryman comes to tend his fire, and starts to see on the now redhot and glowing stones, sunk below the rim, the presentment of a skeleton formed of the purest white ashes —a ghastly spectacle in the grey of the dawn, as the mist rises and the peewit plaintively whistles over the marshy meadow.

CHAPTER VIII

CHURCHYARD PHEASANTS : BEFORE THE BENCH

The tower of the church at Essant Hill was so low that it scarcely seemed to rise above the maples in the hedges. It could not be seen until the last stile in the footpath across the meadows was passed. Church and tower then came into view together on the opposite side of a large open field. A few aged hawthorn trees dotted the sward, and beyond the church the outskirts of a wood were visible, but no dwellings could be seen. Upon a second and more careful glance, however, the chimney of a cottage appeared above a hedge, so covered with ivy as hardly to be separated from the green of the boughs.

There were houses of course somewhere in Essant, but they were so scattered that a stranger might doubt the existence of the village. A few farmsteads long distances apart, and some cottages standing in green lanes and at the corners of the fields, were nearly all ;

there was nothing resembling a ' street '—not so much as a row.   The church was in effect the village, and the church was simply the mausoleum of the Dessant family, the owners of the place.   Essant Hill as a name had been rather a problem to the archæologists, there being no hill : the ground was quite level.   The explanation at last admitted was that Essant Hill was a corruption of D'Essant-ville.

It seemed probable that the population had greatly diminished ; because, although the church was of great antiquity, there was space still for interments in the yard,   A ycw tree of immense size stood in one corner, and was by tradition associated with the for- tunes of the family.   Though the old trunk was much decayed, yet there were still green and flourishing shoots ; so that the superstitious elders said the luck of the house was returning.

Within, the walls of the church were covered with marble slabs, and the space was reduced by the tombs of the Dessants, one with a recumbent figure ; there were two brasses level with the pavement, and in the chancel hung the faded hatchments of the dead. For the pedigree went back to the Battle of Hastings, and there was scarce room for more heraldry. From week's end to week's end the silent nave and aisles remained empty ; the chirp of the sparrows was the only sound

to be heard there. There being no house attached to
the living, the holder could not reside ; so the old
church slumbered in the midst of the meadows, the
hedges, and woods, day after day, year after year.

You could sit on the low churchyard wall in early
summer under the shade of the elms in the hedge,
whose bushes and briars came right over, and listen
to the whistling of the blackbirds or the varied note
of the thrush ; you might see the whitethroat rise and
sing just over the hedge, or look upwards and watch
the swallows and swifts wheeling, wheeling, wheeling
in the sky. No one would pass to disturb your
meditations, whether simply dreaming of nothing in
the genial summer warmth, or thinking over the
course of history since the prows of the Norman ships
grounded on the beach. If we suppose the time, instead of June, to be August or September, there would
not even be the singing of the birds. But as you sat
on the wall, by-and-by the pheasants, tame as chickens,
would come up the hedge and over into the churchyard.

Leaving the church to stroll by the footpath across
the meadow towards the wood, at the first gateway
half-a-dozen more pheasants scatter aside, just far
enough to let you pass. In the short dusty lane more
pheasants ; and again at the edge of the cornfield.

None of these show any signs of alarm, and only move just far enough to avoid being trodden on. Approaching the wood there are yet more pheasants, especially near the fir plantations that come up to the keeper's cottage and form one side of the enclosure of his garden. The pheasants come up to the door to pick up what they can—not long since they were fed there—and then wander away between the slender fir trunks, and beyond them out into the fields.

The path leads presently into a beautiful park, the only defect of which is that it is without undulation. It is quite level ; but still the clumps of noble timber are pleasant to gaze upon. In one spot there still stands the grey wall and buttress of some ancient building, doubtless the relic of an ecclesiastical foundation. The present mansion is not far distant ; it is of large size, but lacks elegance. Inside, nothing that modern skill can supply to render a residence comfortable, convenient, and (as art is understood in furniture) artistic has been neglected.

Behind the fir plantations there is an extensive range of stabling, recently erected, with all the latest improvements. A telegraph wire connects the house with the stable, so that carriage or horse may be instantly summoned. Another wire has been carried to the nearest junction with the general telegraphic system ; so that the resident in this retired spot may communicate his wishes without a moment's delay to any part of the world.

In the gardens and pleasure-grounds near the house all manner of ornamental shrubs are planted. There are conservatories, vineries, pineries ; all the refinements of horticulture. The pheasants stray about the gravel walks and across the close-mown lawn where no daisy dares to lift its head. Yet, with all this precision of luxury, one thing is lacking—*the* one thing, the keystone of English country life—*i.e.* a master whose heart is in the land.

The estate is in process of ' nursing ' for a minor. The revenues had become practically sequestrated to a considerable extent in consequence of careless living when the minor nominally succeeded. It happened that the steward appointed was not only a lawyer of keen intelligence, but a conscientious man. He did his duty thoroughly. Every penny was got out of the estate that could be got, and every penny was saved.

First, the rents were raised to the modern standard, many of them not having been increased for years. Then the tenants were in effect ordered to farm to the highest pitch, and to improve the soil itself by liberal investment. Buildings, drains, and so forth were provided for them ; they only had to pay a small percentage upon the money expended in construction.   In this there was nothing that could be complained of ; but the hard, mechanical, unbending spirit in which it was done—the absence of all kind of sympathy—caused a certain amount of discontent.   The steward next proceeded to turn the mansion, the park, home farm, and preserves into revenue.

Everything was prepared to attract the wealthy man who wanted the temporary use of a good country house, first-class shooting and hunting. He succeeded in doing what few gentlemen have accomplished : he made the pheasants pay.   One reason, of course, was that gentlemen have expenses outside and beyond breeding and keeping : the shooting party itself is expensive ; whereas here the shooting party paid hard cash for their amusement.   The steward had no knowledge of pheasants ; but he had a wide experience of one side of human nature, and he understood accounts.

The keepers were checked by figures at every turn, finding it impossible to elude the businesslike arrangements that were made.   In revenue the result was highly successful.   The mansion with the first-class shooting, hunting, and lovely woodlands—every modern convenience and comfort in the midst of the most rural scenery—let at a high price to good tenants. There was an income from what had previously been profitless. Under this shrewd management the estate was fast recovering.

At the same time the whole parish groaned in spirit. The farmers grumbled at the moral pressure which forced them to progress in spite of themselves. They grumbled at the strange people who took up their residence in their midst and suddenly claimed all the loyalty which was the due of the old family. These people hunted over their fields, jumped over the hedges, glanced at them superciliously, and seemed astonished if every hat was not raised when they came in sight. The farmers felt that they were regarded as ignorant barbarians, and resented the town-bred insolence of people who aped the country gentleman.

They grumbled about the over-preservation of game, and they grumbled about the rabbits. The hunt had its grumble too because some of the finest coverts were closed to the hounds, and because they wanted to know what became of the foxes that formerly lived in those coverts. Here was a beautiful place—a place that one might dream life away in —filled with all manner of discontent.

Everything was done with the best intention. But the keystone was wanting—the landlord, the master, who had grown up in the traditions of the

spot, and between whom and the people there would
have been, even despite of grievances, a certain
amount of sympathy. So true is it that in England,
under the existing system of land tenure, an estate
cannot be worked like the machinery of a factory.

At first, when the pheasant-preserving began to
reach such a height, there was a great deal of poaching by the resident labourers. The temptation was
thrust so closely before their faces they could not
resist it. When pheasants came wandering into the
cottage gardens, and could even be enticed into the
sheds and so secured by simply shutting the door,
men who would not have gone out of their way to
poach were led to commit themselves.

There followed a succession of prosecutions and
fines, till the place began to get a reputation for that
sort of thing. It was at last intimated to the steward
by certain gentlemen that this course of prosecution
was extremely injudicious. For it is a fact—a fact
carefully ignored sometimes—that resident gentlemen
object to prosecutions, and, so far from being anxious
to fine or imprison poachers, would very much rather
not. The steward took the hint, and instead increased
his watchers. But by this time the novelty of pheasants roaming about like fowls had begun to wear off,
and their services were hardly needed. Men went by

pheasants with as much indifference as they would pass a tame duck by the roadside.

Such poachers as visited the woods came from a distance. Two determined raids were carried out by strangers, who escaped. Every now and then wires were found that had been abandoned, but the poaching ceased to be more than is usual on most properties. So far as the inhabitants of the parish were concerned it almost ceased altogether; but every now and then the strollers, gipsies, and similar characters carried off a pheasant or a hare, or half a dozen rabbits. These offenders when detected were usually charged before the Bench at a market town not many miles distant. Let us follow one there.

The little town of L——, which has not even a branch railway, mainly consists of a long street. In one part this street widens out, so that the houses are some forty yards or more apart, and it then again contracts. This irregularly shaped opening is the market-place, and here in the centre stands a rude-looking building. It is supported upon thick short pillars, and was perhaps preceded by a wooden structure. Under these pillars there is usually a shabby chaise or two run in for cover, and the spot is the general rendezvous of all the dogs in the town.

This morning there are a few loafers hanging

round the place ; and the tame town pigeons have fluttered down, and walk with nodding heads almost up to them. These pigeons always come to the edge of a group of people, mindful of the stray grain and peas that fall from the hands of farmers and dealers examining samples on market days. Presently, two constables come across carrying a heavy, clumsy box between them. They unlock a door, and take the box upstairs into the hall over the pillars. After them saunters a seedy man, evidently a clerk, with a rusty black bag ; and after him again—for the magistrates' Clerk's clerk must have *his* clerk—a boy with some leather-bound books.

Some of the loafers touch their hats as a gentleman—a magistrate—rides up the street. But although the church clock is striking the hour fixed for the sessions to begin he does not come over to the hall upon dismounting in the inn-yard, but quietly strolls away to transact some business with the wine-merchant or the saddler. There really is not the least hurry. The Clerk stands in the inn porch calmly enjoying the September sunshine, and chatting with the landlord. Two or three more magistrates drive up ; presently the chairman strolls over on foot from his house, which is almost in the town, to the inn, and joins in the pleasant gossip going on there, of course in a private apartment.

Up in the justice-room the seedy Clerk's clerk is leaning out of the window and conversing with a man below who has come along with a barrow-load of vegetables from his allotment. Some boys are spinning tops under the pillars. On the stone steps that lead up to the hall a young mother sits nursing her infant ; she is waiting to 'swear' the child. In the room itself several gipsy-looking men and women lounge in a corner. At one end is a broad table and some comfortable chairs behind it. In front of each chair, on the table, two sheets of clean foolscap have been placed on a sheet of blotting-paper. These and a variety of printed forms were taken from the clumsy box that is now open.

At last there is a slight stir as a group is seen to emerge from the inn, and the magistrates take their seats. An elderly man who sits by the chair cocks his felt hat on the back of his head : the clerical magistrate very tenderly places his beaver in safety on the broad mantelpiece, that no irreverent sleeve may ruffle its gloss : several others who rarely do more than nod assent range themselves on the flanks ; one younger man who looks as if he understood horses pulls out his toothpick. The chairman, stout and gouty, seizes a quill and sternly looks over the list of cases.

Half a dozen summonses for non-payment of rates come first ; then a dispute between a farmer and his man.   After this the young mother ' swears ' her child ; and, indeed, there is some very hard swearing here on both sides.   A wrangle between two women —neighbours—who accuse each other of assault, and scream and chatter their loudest, comes next.   Before they decide it, the Bench retire, and are absent a long time.

By degrees a buzz arises, till the justice-room is as noisy as a market.   Suddenly the door of the private room opens, and the Clerk comes out ; instantly the buzz subsides, and in the silence those who are nearest catch something about the odds and the St. Leger, and an anything but magisterial roar of laughter. The chairman appears, rigidly compressing his features, and begins to deliver his sentence before he can sit down, but the solemn effect is much marred by the passing of a steam ploughing engine.   The audience, too, tend away towards the windows to see whose engine it is.

' Silence ! ' cries the Clerk, who has himself been looking out of window ; the shuffling of feet ceases, and it is found that after this long consultation the Bench have dismissed both charges.   The next case on the list is poaching ; and at the call of his name one of the gipsy-looking men advances, and is ordered to stand before that part of the table which by consent represents the bar.

'Oby Bottleton,' says the Clerk, half reading, half extemporizing, and shuffling his papers to conceal certain slips of technicality; 'you are charged with trespassing in pursuit of game at Essant Hill—that you did use a wire on the estate—on land in the occupation of Johnson.'—'It's a lie!' cries a good-looking, dark-complexioned woman, who has come up behind the defendant (the whilome navvy), and carries a child so wrapped in a shawl as to be invisible. 'Silence! or you'll have to go outside the court. Mr. Dalton Dessant will leave the Bench during the hearing of this case.' Mr. Dalton Dessant, one of the silent magistrates already alluded to, bows to the chairman, and wriggles his chair back about two feet from the table. There he gazes at the ceiling. He is one of the trustees of the Essant Hill property; and the Bench are very careful to consult public opinion in L—— borough.

The first witness is an assistant keeper: the head keeper stands behind him—a fine man, still upright and hearty-looking, but evidently at the beginning of the vale of years; he holds his hat in his hand; the sunlight falls through the casement on his worn velveteen jacket. The assistant, with the aid of a few questions from the Clerk, gives his evidence very clear and fairly. ' I saw the defendant's van go down the lane,' he says :

' It bean't my van,' interrupts the defendant ; ' it's my brother's.'

' You'll have an opportunity of speaking presently,' says the Clerk. ' Go on ' (to the witness).

' After the van went down the lane, it stopped by the highway-road, and the horse was taken out. The women left the van with baskets, and went towards the village.'

' Yes, yes ; come to the point. Did you hide your-self by order of the head keeper ? '

' I did—in the nutwood hedge by Three Corner Piece ; after a bit I saw the defendant.'

' Had you any reason for watching there ? '

' There was a wire and a rabbit in it.'

' Well, what happened ? '

' I waited a long time, and presently the defend-ant got over the gate. He was very particular not to step on the soft mud by the gate—he kind of leaped over it, not to leave the mark of his boots. He had a lurcher with him, and I was afraid the dog would scent me in the hedge.'

' You rascal ! ' (from the defendant's wife).

'But he didn't, and, after looking carefully round, the defendant picked up the rabbit, and put it and the wire in his pocket.'

'What did you do then?'

'I got out of the hedge and came towards him. Directly he saw me he ran across the field; I whistled as loud as I could, and he' (jerking a thumb back towards the head-keeper) 'came out of the firs into the lane and stopped him. We found the wire and the rabbit in his pocket, and two more wires. I produce the wires.'

This was the sum of the evidence; the head-keeper simply confirmed the latter part of it. Oby replied that it was all false from beginning to end. He had not got corduroy trousers on that day, as stated. He was not there at all: he was in the village, and he could call witnesses to prove it. The Clerk reminded the audience that there was such a thing as imprisonment for perjury.

Then the defendant turned savagely on the first witness, and admitted the truth of his statement by asking what he said when collared in the lane. 'You said you had had a good lot lately, and didn't care if you was nailed this time.'

'Oh, what awful lies!' cried the wife. 'It's a wonder you don't fall dead!'

'You were not there,' the Clerk remarked quietly. 'Now, Oby, what is your defence? Have you got any witnesses?'

'No; I ain't got no witnesses. All as I did, I know I walked up the hedge to look for mushrooms. I saw one of them things '—meaning the wires on the table—'and I just stooped down to see what it was, 'cos I didn't know. I never seed one afore; and I was just going to pick it up and look at it' (the magistrates glance at each other, and cannot suppress a smile at this profound innocence), 'when this fellow jumped out and frightened me. I never seed no rabbit.'

'Why, you put the rabbit in your pocket,' interrupts the first witness.

'Never mind,' said the Clerk to the witness; 'let him go on.'

'That's all as I got to say,' continues the defendant. 'I never seed no such things afore; and if he hadn't come I should have put it down again.'

'But you were trespassing,' said the Clerk.

'I didn't know it. There wasn't no notice-board.'

'Now, Oby,' cried the head-keeper, 'you know you've been along that lane this ten years.'

'That will do' (from the chairman); 'is there any more evidence?'

As none was forthcoming, the Bench turned a little aside and spoke in low tones. The defendant's wife immediately set up a sobbing, varied occasionally by a shriek; the infant woke up and cried, and two or three women of the same party behind began to talk in excited tones about 'Shame.' The sentence was 2*l.* and costs—an announcement that caused a perfect storm of howling and crying.

The defendant put his hands in his pockets with the complacent expression of a martyr. 'I must go to gaol a' spose; none of ourn ever went thur afore: a' spose *I* must go.' 'Come,' said the Clerk, 'why, you or your brother bought a piece of land and a cottage not long ago,'—then to the Bench, 'They're not real gipsies: he is a grandson of old Bottleton who had the tollgate; you recollect, Sir.'

But the defendant declares he has no money; his friends shake their heads gloomily; and amid the shrieking of his wife and the crying of the child he is removed in the custody of two constables, to be presently conveyed to gaol. With ferocious glances at the Bench, as if they would like to tear the chairman's eyes out, the women leave the court.

'Next case,' calls the Clerk. The court sits about two hours longer, having taken some five hours to get through six cases. Just as the chairman rises the poacher's wife returns to the table, without her child, angrily pulls out a dirty canvas bag, and throws down three or four sovereigns before the seedy Clerk's clerk. The canvas bag is evidently half-full of money —the gleam of silver and gold is visible within it· The Bench stay to note this proceeding with an amused expression on their features. The woman looks at them as bold as brass, and stalks off with her man.

Half an hour afterwards, two of the magistrates riding away from the town pass a small tavern on the outskirts. A travelling van is outside, and from the chimney on its roof thin smoke arises. There is a little group at the doorway, and among them stands the late prisoner. Oby holds a foaming tankard in one hand, and touches his battered hat, as the magis· trates go by, with a gesture of sly humility.

CHAPTER IX

LUKE, THE RABBIT CONTRACTOR: THE BROOK-PATH

THE waggon-track leading to the Upper Woods almost always presented something of interest, and often of beauty. The solitude of the place seemed to have attracted flowers and ferns as well as wild animals and birds. For though flowers have no power of motion, yet seeds have a negative choice and lie dormant where they do not find a kindly welcome. But those carried hither by the birds or winds took root and flourished, secure from the rude ploughshare or the sharp scythe.

The slow rumble of waggon-wheels seldom disturbed the dreamy silence, or interrupted the song of the birds ; so seldom that large docks and thistles grew calmly beside the ruts untouched by hoofs. From the thick hedges on either side trailing brambles and briars stretched far out, and here and there was a fallen branch, broken off by the winds, whose leaves had turned brown and withered while all else was green. Round sarsen stones had been laid down in the marshy places to form a firm road, but the turf had long since covered most of them. Where the smooth brown surfaces did project mosses had lined the base, and rushes leaned over and hid the rest.

In the ditches, under the shade of the brambles, the hart's-tongue fern extended its long blade of dark glossy green. By the decaying stoles the hardy fern flourished, under the trees on the mounds the lady fern could be found, and farther up nearer the wood the tall brake almost supplanted the bushes. Oak and ash boughs reached across: in the ash the wood-pigeons lingered. Every now and then the bright colours of the green woodpeckers flashed to and fro their nest in a tree hard by. They would not have chosen it had not the place been nearly as quiet as the wood itself.

Blackthorn bushes jealously encroached on the narrow stile that entered the lane from a meadow— a mere rail thrust across a gap. The gates, set in deep recesses—short lanes themselves cut through the mounds—were rotten and decayed, so as to scarcely hold together, and not to be moved without

care. Hawthorn branches on each side pushed
forward and lessened the opening ; on the ground,
where the gateposts had rotted nearly off, fungi came
up in thick bunches.

The little meadows to which they led were rich in
oaks, growing on the 'shore' of the ditches, tree after
tree. The grass in them was not plentiful, but the
flowers were many ; in the spring the orchis sent up
its beautiful purple, and in the heat of summer the
bird's-foot lotus flourished in the sunny places.
Farther up, nearer the wood, the lane became
hollow—worn down between high banks, at first
clothed with fern, and then, as the hill got steeper,
with fir trees.

Where firs are tall and thick together the sunbeams that fall aslant between them seem to be made
more visible than under other trees, by the motes or
wood dust in the air. Still farther the banks became
even steeper, till nothing but scanty ash stoles could
grow upon them, the fir plantations skirting along the
summit. Then suddenly, at a turn, the ground sank
into a deep hollow, where in spring the eye rested
with relief and pleasure on the tops of young firs, acre
after acre, just freshly tinted with the most delicate
green. From thence the track went into the wood.

By day all through the summer months there was

always something to be seen in the lane—a squirrel, a stoat; always a song-bird to listen to, a flower or fern to gather. By night the goatsucker visited it, and the bat, and the white owl gliding down the slope. In winter when the clouds hung low the darkness in the hollow between the high banks, where the light was shut out by the fir trees, was like that of a cavern. It was then that night after night a strange procession wended down it.

First came an old man, walking stiffly—not so much from age as rheumatism—and helping his unsteady steps on the slippery sarsen stones with a stout ground-ash staff. Behind him followed a younger man, and in the rear a boy. Sometimes there was an extra assistant, making four ; sometimes there was only the old man and one companion. Each had a long and strong ash stick across his shoulder, on which a load of rabbits was slung, an equal number in front and behind, to balance. The old fellow, who was dressed shabbily even for a labourer, was the contractor for the rabbits shot or ferreted in these woods.

He took the whole number at a certain fixed price all round, and made what he could out of them. Every evening in the season he went to the woods to fetch those that had been captured during the day, conveying them to his cottage on the outskirts of the village. From thence they went by carrier's cart to the railway. Old Luke's books, such as they were, were quite beyond the understanding of any one but himself and his wife ; nor could even they themselves tell you exactly how many dozen he purchased in the year. But in his cups the wicked old hypocrite had often been known to boast that he paid the lord of the manor as much money as the rent of a small farm.

One of Luke's eyes was closed with a kind of watery rheum, and was never opened except when he thought a rabbit was about to jump into a net. The other was but half open, and so overhung with a thick grey eyebrow as to be barely visible. His cheeks were the hue of clay, his chin scrubby, and a lanky black forelock depended over one temple. A battered felt hat, a ragged discoloured slop, and corduroys stained with the clay of the banks completed his squalid costume.

A more miserable object or one apparently more deserving of pity it would be hard to imagine. To see him crawl with slow and feeble steps across the fields in winter, gradually working his way in the teeth of a driving rain, was enough to arouse compassion in the hardest heart : there was something so utterly woe-begone in his whole aspect—so weather-beaten, as if he had been rained upon ever since childhood. He seemed humbled to the ground—crushed and spiritless.

Now and then Luke was employed by some of the farmers to do their ferreting for them and to catch the rabbits in the banks by the roadside. More than once benevolent people driving by in their cosy cushioned carriages, and seeing this lonely wretch in the bitter wind watching a rabbit's hole as if he were a dog well beaten and thrashed, had been known to stop and call the poor old fellow to the carriage door. Then Luke would lay his hand on his knee, shake his head, and sorrowfully state his pains and miseries : ' Aw, I be ter-rable bad, I be,' he would say; 'I be most terrable bad : I can't but just drag my leg out of this yer ditch. It be a dull job, bless 'ee, this yer.' The tone, the look of the man, the dreary winter landscape all so thoroughly agreed together that a few small silver coins would drop into his hand, and Luke, with a deep groaning sigh of thankfulness, would bow and scrape and go back to his ' dull job.'

Luke, indeed, somehow or other was always in favour with the 'quality.' He was as firmly fixed in his business as if he had been the most clever courtier.

It was not of the least use for any one else to offer to take the rabbits, even if they would give more money. No, Luke was the trusty man; Luke, and nobody else, was worthy. So he grovelled on from year to year, blinking about the place. When some tenant found a gin in the turnip field, or a wire by the clover, and quietly waited till Luke came fumbling by and picked up the hare or rabbit, it did not make the slightest difference though he went straight to the keeper and made a formal statement.

Luke had an answer always ready : he had not set the wire, but had stumbled on it unawares, and was going to take it to the keeper; or he had noticed a colony of rats about, and had put the gin for them. Now, the same excuse might have been made by any other poacher ; the difference lay in this—that Luke was believed. At all events, such little trifles were forgotten, and Luke went on as before. He did a good deal of the ferreting in the hedges outside the woods himself : if he took home three dozen from the mound and only paid for two dozen, that scarcely concerned the world at large.

If in coming down the dark and slippery lane at night somebody with a heavy sack stepped out from the shadow at the stile, and if the contents of the sack were rapidly transferred to the shoulder-sticks, or the bag itself bodily taken along—why, there was nobody there to see. As for the young man and the boy who helped, those discreet persons had always a rabbit for their own pot, or even for a friend ; and indeed it was often remarked that old Luke could always get plenty of men to work for him. No one ever hinted at searching the dirty shed at the side of his cottage that was always locked by day, or looking inside the disused oven that it covered. But if fur or feathers had been found there, was not he the contractor? And clearly if a pheasant *was* there he could not be held· responsible for the unauthorised acts of his assistants.

The truth was that Luke was the most thorough-paced poacher in the place—or, rather, he was a wholesale receiver. His success lay in making it pleasant for everybody all round. It was pleasant for the keeper, who could always dispose of a few hares or pheasants if he wanted a little money. The keeper, in ways known to himself, made it pleasant for the bailiff. It was equally pleasant for the under-keepers, who had what they wanted (in reason), and enjoyed a little by-play on their own account. It was pleasant for his men ; and it was pleasant—specially pleasant— at a little wayside inn kept by Luke's nephew, and, as **was** believed, with Luke's money. Everybody concerned in the business could always procure refreshment there, including the policeman.

There was only one class of persons whom Luke could not conciliate; and they were the tenants. These very inconsiderate folk argued that it was the keepers' and Luke's interest to maintain a very large stock of rabbits, which meant great inroads on their crops. There seemed to be even something like truth in their complaints; and once or twice the more independent carried their grievances to headquarters so effectual'y as to elicit an order for the destruction of the rabbits forthwith on their farms. But of what avail was such an order when the execution of it was entrusted to Luke himself?

In time the tenants got to put up with Luke; and the wiser of them turned round and tried to make it still more pleasant for *him* : they spoke a good word for him ; they gave him a quart of ale, and put little things in his way, such as a chance to buy and sell faggots at a small profit. Not to be ungrateful, Luke kept their rabbits within reasonable bounds ; and he had this great recommendation—that whether they bullied him or whether they gave him ale and bread-and-cheese, Luke was always humble and always touched his hat.

His wife kept a small shop for the sale of the

coarser groceries and a little bacon.   He had also
rather extensive gardens, from which he sold quantities
of vegetables.   It was more than suspected that the
carrier's cart was really Luke's—that is, he found the
money for horsing it, and could take possession if he
liked. The carrier's cart took his rabbits, and the game
he purchased of poachers, to the railway, and the vegetables from the gardens to the customers in town.

At least one cottage besides his own belonged to
him ; and some would have it that this was one of the
reasons of his success with the 'quality.'   The people
at the great house, anxious to increase their influence,
wished to buy every cottage and spare piece of land.
This was well known, and many small owners prided
themselves upon spiting the big people at the great
house by refusing to sell, or selling to another person.
The great house was believed to have secured the first
'refuse' of Luke's property, if ever he thought of selling.
Luke, in fact, among the lower classes was looked
upon as a capitalist—a miser with an unknown hoard.
The old man used to sit of a winter's evening, after he
had brought down the rabbits, by the hearth, making
rabbit-nets of twine. Almost everybody who came
along the road, home from the market town, stopped,
lifted the latch without knocking, and looked in to tell
the news or hear it.   But Luke's favourite manœuvre

was to take out his snuff-box, tap it, and offer it to
the person addressing him. This he would do to a
farmer, even though it were the largest tenant of all.
For this snuff-box was a present from the lady at the
great house, who took an interest in poor old Luke's
infirmities, and gave him the snuff-box, a really good
piece of workmanship, well filled with the finest snuff,
to console his wretchedness.

Of this box Luke was as proud as if it had been
the insignia of the Legion of Honour, and never lost
an opportunity of showing it to every one of standing.
When the village heard of this kindly present it ran
over in its mind all that it knew about the stile, and
the sacks, and the disused oven. Then the village
very quietly shrugged its shoulders, and though it
knew not the word irony, well understood what that
term conveys.

At the foot of the hill on which the Upper Woods
were situate there extended a level tract of meadows
with some cornfields. Through these there flowed a
large slow brook, often flooded in winter by the water
rushing down from the higher lands. It was pleasant
in the early year to walk now and then along the
footpath that followed the brook, noting the gradual
changes in the hedges.

When the first swallow of the spring wheels over

the watery places the dry sedges of last year still stand as they grew.   They are supported by the bushes beside the meadow ditch where it widens to join the brook, and the water it brings down from the furrows scarcely moves through the belt of willow lining the larger stream.   As the soft west wind runs· along the hedge it draws a sigh from the dead dry stalks and leaves that will no more feel the rising sap.

By the wet furrows the ground has still a brownish tint, for there the floods lingered and discoloured the grass.   Near the ditch pointed flags are springing up, and the thick stems of the marsh marigold.   From bunches of dark green leaves slender stalks arise and bear the golden petals of the marsh buttercups, the lesser celandine.   If the wind blows cold and rainy they will close, and open again to the sunshine.

At the outside of the withies, where the earth is drier, stand tall horse-chestnut trees, aspen, and beech. The leaflets of the horse-chestnut are already opening ; but on the ground, half-hidden under beech leaves not yet decayed, and sycamore leaves reduced to imperfect grey skeletons, there lies a chestnut shell.   It is sodden, and has lost its original green—the prickles, too, have decayed and disappeared ; yet at a touch it falls apart, and discloses two chestnuts, still of a rich, deep polished brown.

On the very bank of the brook there grows a beech whose bare boughs droop over, almost dipping in the water, where it comes with a swift rush from the narrow arches of a small bridge whose bricks are green with moss. The current is still slightly turbid, for the floods have not long subsided, and the soaked meadows and ploughed fields send their rills to swell the brook and stain it with sand and earth. On the surface float down twigs and small branches forced from the trees by the gales : sometimes an entangled mass of aquatic weeds—long, slender green filaments twisted and matted together—comes more slowly because heavy and deep in the water.

A little bird comes flitting silently from the willows and perches on the drooping beech branch. It is a delicate little creature, the breast of a faint and dull yellowy green, the wings the lightest brown, and there is a pencilled streak over the eye. The beak is so slender it scarce seems capable of the work it should do, the legs and feet so tiny that they are barely visible. Hardly has he perched than the keen eyes detect a small black speck that has just issued from the arch, floating fast on the surface of the stream and borne round and round in a tiny whirlpool.

He darts from the branch, hovers just above the water, and in a second has seized the black speck and

returned to the branch.   A moment or two passes, and
again he darts down and takes something—this time
invisible—from the water.   A third time he hovers,
and on this occasion just brushes the surface.   Then,
suddenly finding that these movements are watched
he flits—all too soon—up high into the beech and
away into the narrow copse.   The general tint and
shape of the bird are those of the willow wren, but it
is difficult to identify the species in so brief a glance
and without hearing its note.

The path now trends somewhat away from the
stream and skirts a ploughed field, where the hedges
are cropped close and the elms stripped of the lesser
boughs about the trunks, that the sparrows may not
find shelter.   But all the same there are birds here
too—one in the thick low hedge, two or three farther
on, another in the ditch perching on the dead white
stems of last year's plants that can hardly support
an ounce weight, and all calling to each other.   It is
six marsh-tits, as busy as they can well be.

One rises from the ditch to the trunk of an elm
where the thick bark is green with lichen : he goes up
the tree like a woodpecker, and peers into every
crevice.   His little beak strikes, peck, peck, at a
place where something is hidden : then he proceeds
farther up the trunk : next he descends a few steps

in a sidelong way, and finally hops down some three
inches head foremost, and alights again on the all but
perpendicular bark.   But his tail does not touch the
tree, and in another minute down he flies again to
the ditch.

A shrill and yet low note that sounds something
like 'skeek-skeek' comes from a birch, and another
'skeek-skeek' answers from an elm.   It is like the
friction of iron against iron without oil on the bearings.
This is the tree-climber calling to his mate.   He
creeps over the boles of the birch, and where the
larger limbs join the trunk, trailing his tail along the
bark, and clinging so closely that but for the sharp
note he would be passed.   Even when that has called
attention the colour of his back so little differs from
the colour of bark that if he is some height up the
tree it is not easy to detect him.

The days go on and the hedges become green—
the sun shines, and the blackbirds whistle in the trees.
They leave the hedge, and mount into the elm or ash
to deliver their song ; then, after a pause, dive down
again to the bushes.   Up from the pale green corn
that is yet but a few inches high rises a little brown
bird, mounting till he has attained to the elevation
of the adjacent oak.   Then, beginning his song, he
extends his wings, lifts his tail, and gradually descends

slanting forward—slowly, like a parachute—sing, sing, singing all the while till the little legs, that can be seen against the sky somewhat depending, touch the earth and the wheat hides him. Still from the clod comes the finishing bar of his music.

In a short time up he rises again, and this time from the summit of his flight sinks in a similar manner singing to a branch of the oak. There he sings again ; and, again rising, comes back almost to the same bough singing as he descends. But he is not alone : from an elm hard by come the same notes, and from yet another tree they are also re-peated. They cannot rest—now one flits from the topmost bough of an elm to another topmost bough ; now a second comes up from feeding, and cries from the branches. They are tree-pipits ; and though the call is monotonous, yet it is so cheerful and pleasing that one cannot choose but stay and listen.

Suddenly, two that have been vigorously calling start forward together and meet in mid-air. They buffet each other with their wings ; their little beaks fiercely strike ; their necks are extended ; they manœuvre round each other, trying for an advantage. They descend, heedless in the rage of their tiny hearts, within a few yards of the watcher, and then

·in alarm separate.   But one flies to the oak branch and defiantly calls immediately.

Over the meadows comes the distant note of the cuckoo.   When he first calls his voice is short and somewhat rough, but in a few days it gains power. Then the second syllable has a mellow ring : and as he cries from the tree, the note, swiftly repeated and echoed by the wood, dwells on the ear something like the 'hum' or vibration of a beautiful bell.

As the hedges become green the ivy leaves turn brown at the edge and fall ; the wild ivy is often curiously variegated.   At the foot of the tree up which it climbs the leaves are five-angled, higher up they lose the angles and become rounded, though growing on the same plant.   Sometimes they have a grey tint, especially those that trail along the bank ; sometimes the leaves are a reddish brown with pale green ribs.

By the brook now the meadow has become of a rich bright green, the stream has sunk and is clear, and the sunlight dances on the ripples.   The grasses at the edge—the turf—curl over and begin to grow down the steep side that a little while since was washed by the current.   Where there is a ledge of mud and sand the yellow wagtail runs ; he stands on a stone and jerks his tail.

The ploughed field that comes down almost to the brook—a mere strip of meadow between—is green too with rising wheat, high enough now to hide the partridges. Before it got so tall it was pleasant to watch the pair that frequent it ; they were so confident that they did not even trouble to cower. At any other time of year they would have run, or flown ; but then, though scarcely forty yards away and perfectly visible, they simply ceased feeding but showed no further alarm.

Upon the plough birds in general should look as their best friend, for it provides them with the staff of life as much as it does man. The earth turned up under the share yields them grubs and insects and worms : the seed is sown and the clods harrowed, and they take a second toll ; the weeds are hoed or pulled up, and at their roots there are more insects ; from the stalk and ears and the bloom of the rising corn they seize caterpillars ; when it is ripe they enjoy the grain ; when it is cut and carried there are ears in the stubble, and they can then feast on the seeds of the innumerable plants that flowered among it ; finally comes the plough again. It is as if the men and horses worked for the birds.

The horse-chestnut trees in the narrow copse bloom ; the bees are humming everywhere and summer is at hand. Presently the brown cockchafers will come almost like an army of locusts, as suddenly appearing without a sign. They seem to be particularly numerous where there is much maple in the hedges.

Resting now on the sward by the stream—contracted in seeming by the weeds and flags and fresh sedges—there comes the distant murmur of voices and the musical laugh of girls. The ear tries to distinguish the words and gather the meaning ; but the syllables are intertangled—it is like listening to a low sweet song in a language all unknown. This is the water falling gently over the mossy hatch and splashing faintly on the stones beneath ; the blue dragon-flies dart over the smooth surface or alight on a broad leaf —these blue dragon-flies when thus resting curl the tail upwards.

Farther up above the mere there is a spot where the pool itself ends, or rather imperceptibly disappears among a vast mass of aquatic weeds. To these on the soft oozy mud succeed acres of sedge and rush and great tufts of greyish grass. Low willows are scattered about, and alder at the edge and where the ground is firmer. This is the home of the dragon-flies, of the coots, whose white bald foreheads distinguish them at a distance, and of the moorhens.

A narrow lane crosses it on a low bank or cause-way but just raised above the level of the floods. It is bordered on either side by thick hawthorn hedges, and these again are further rendered more impassable by the rankest growth of hemlocks, 'gicks,' nettles, hedge-parsley, and similar coarse plants. In these the nettle-creeper (white-throat) hides her nest, and they have so encroached that the footpath is almost threatened. This lane leads from the Upper Woods across the marshy level to the cornfields, being a branch from that down which Luke the contractor carried his rabbits.

Now a hare coming from the uplands beyond the woods, or from the woods, and desirous of visiting the cornfields of the level grounds below, found it difficult to pass the water. For besides the marsh itself, the mere, and the brook, another slow, stagnant stream, quite choked with sedges and flags, uncut for years, ran into it, or rather joined it, and before doing so meandered along the very foot of the hill-side over which the woods grew. To a hare or a rabbit, there-fore, there was but one path or exit without taking to the water in this direction for nearly a mile, and that was across this narrow raised causeway. The pheasants frequently used it, as if preferring to walk than to fly. Partridges came too, to seat themselves in the dry dust—a thing they do daily in warm weather.

Hares were constantly passing from the cornfields to the wood, and the wood to the cornfields ; and they had another reason for using this track, because so many herbs and plants, whose leaves they like better than grass, flourished at the sides of the hedges. No scythe cuts them down, as it does by the hedges in the meadows ; nor was a man sent round with a reaping-hook to chop them off, as is often done round the arable fields. There was, therefore, always a feast here, to which, also, the rabbits came.

The poachers were perfectly well aware of all this, and as a consequence this narrow lane became a most favourite haunt of theirs. A wire set in the runs that led to the causeway, or in the causeway itself, was almost certain to be thrown. At one time it was occasionally netted ; and now and then a bolder fellow hid himself in the bushes with a gun, and took his choice of pheasant, partridge, hare, or rabbit. These practices were possible, because, although so secluded, there was a public right-of-way along the lane.

But of recent years, as game became more valued and the keepers were increased, a check was put upon it, though even now wires are frequently found which poachers have been obliged to abandon. They are loth to give up a place that has a kind of poaching reputation. As if in revenge for the interference, they have so ransacked the marsh every spring for the eggs of the waterfowl that the wild duck will not lay there, but seek spots safer from such enemies. The marsh is left to the coots and moorhens that from thence stock the brooks

CHAPTER X

FARMER WILLUM'S PLACE : SNIPE SHOOTING

ONE October morning towards the end of the month, Orion and I started to beat over Redcote Farm upon the standing invitation of the occupier. There was a certainty of sport of some kind, because the place had remained almost unchanged for the last century. It is 'improvement' that drives away game and necessitates the pheasant preserve.

The low whitewashed walls of the house were of a dull yellowish hue from the beating of the weather. They supported a vast breadth of thatched roof drilled by sparrows and starlings. Under the eaves the swallows' nests adhered, and projecting shelves were fixed to prevent any inconvenience from them. Some of the narrow windows were still darkened with the black boarding put up in the days of the window tax.

In the courtyard a number of stout forked stakes

were used for putting the dairy buckets on, after being
cleaned, to dry.   No attempt was made to separate
the business from the inner life of the house.   Here
in front these oaken buckets, scoured till nearly white,
their iron handles polished like silver, were close
under the eyes of any one looking out.   By the front
door a besom leaned against the wall that every
comer might clean the mud from his boots ; and **you**
stepped at once from the threshold into the sitting-
room.   A lane led past the garden, if that could be
called a lane which widened into a field and after rain
was flooded so deeply as to be impassable to foot
passengers.

The morning we had chosen was fine ; and, after
shaking hands with old Farmer 'Willum,' whose
shooting days were over, we entered the lane, and by
it the fields.   The meadows were small, enclosed with
double-mounds, and thickly timbered, so that as the
ground was level you could not see beyond the field
in which you stood, and upon looking over the gate
might surprise a flock of pigeons, a covey of partridges, or a rabbit out feeding.   Though the tinted
leaves were fast falling, the hedges where still full of
plants and vegetation that prevented seeing through
them.   The ' kuck-kuck ' of the redwings came from
the bushes—the first note of approaching winter—and

the tips of the rushes were dead. Red haws on the
hawthorn and hips on the briar sprinkled the hedge
with bright spots of colour.

The two spaniels went with such an eager rush
into a thick double-mound, dashing heedlessly through
the nettles and under the brambles, that we hastened
to get one on each side of the hedge. A rustling—
a short bark; another, then a movement among the
rushes in the ditch, evidently not made by the dogs;
then a silence. But the dogs come back, and as they
give tongue the rabbit rushes past a bare spot on the
slope of the bank. I fire—a snap shot—and cut out
some fur, but do no further harm; the pellets bury
themselves in the earth. But, startled and perhaps just
stung by a stray shot, the rabbit bolts fairly at last
twenty yards in front of Orion, the spaniel tearing at
his heels.

Up goes the double-barrel with a bright gleam as
the sunlight glances on it. A second of suspense:
then from the black muzzle darts a cylinder of tawny
flame and an opening cone of white smoke: a sharp
report rings on the ear. The rabbit rolls over and
over, and is dead before the dog can seize him. After
harling the rabbit, Orion hangs him high on a projecting branch, so that the man who is following us
at a distance may easily find the game. He is a

labourer, and we object to have him with us, as we know he would be certain to get in the way.

We then tried a corner where two of these large mounds, meeting, formed a small copse in which grew a quantity of withy and the thick grasses that always border the stoles.   A hare bolted almost directly the dogs went in : hares trust in their speed, rabbits in doubling for cover.   I fired right and left, and missed : fairly missed with both barrels.   Orion jumped upon the mound from the other side, and from that elevation sent a third cartridge after her.

It was a long, a very long shot, but the hare perceptibly winced.   Still, she drew easily away from the dogs, going straight for a distant gateway.   But before it was reached the pace slackened ; she made ineffectual attempts to double as the slow spaniels overtook her, but her strength was ebbing, and they quickly ran in.   Reloading, and in none of the best of tempers, I followed the mound.   The miss was of course the gun's fault—it was foul ; or the cartridges, or the bad quality of the powder.

We passed the well-remembered hollow ash pollard, whence, years before, we had taken the young owls, and in which we had hidden the old single-barrel gun one sultry afternoon when it suddenly came on to thunder.   The flashes were so vivid and the discharges seemingly so near that we became afraid to hold the gun, knowing that metal attracted electricity. So it was put in the hollow tree out ot the wet, and with it the powder-flask, while we crouched under an adjacent hawthorn till the storm ceased.

Then by the much-patched and heavy gate where I shot my first snipe, that rose out of the little stream and went straight up over the top bar. The emotion, for it was more than excitement, of that moment will never pass from memory. It was the bird of all others that I longed to kill, and certainly to a lad the most difficult. Day after day I went down into the water-meadows; first thinking over the problem of the snipe's peculiar twisting flight. At one time I determined that I would control the almost irresistible desire to fire till the bird had completed his burst of zig-zag and settled to something like a straight line. At another I as firmly resolved to shoot the moment the snipe rose before he could begin to twist. But some unforeseen circumstance always interfered with the execution of these resolutions.

Now the snipe got up unexpectedly right under foot; now one rose thirty yards ahead; now he towered straight up, forced to do so by the tall willows; and occasionally four or five rising together and

calling 'sceap, sceap' in as many different directions,
made me hesitate at which to aim. The continual
dwelling upon the problem rendered me nervous, so
that I scarcely knew when I pulled the trigger.

But one day, in passing this gateway, which was
a long distance from the particular water-meadows
where I had practised, and not thinking of snipes,
suddenly one got up, and with a loud 'sceap' darted
over the gate. The long slender gun—the old single-
barrel—came to the shoulder instinctively, without
premeditation, and the snipe fell.

Coming now to the brook, which was broad and
bordered by a hedge on the opposite side, I held
Orion's gun while he leaped over. The bank was
steep and awkward, but he had planned his leap so
as to alight just where he could at once grasp an ash
branch and so save himself from falling back into the
water. He could not, however, stay suspended there,
but had to scramble over the hedge, and then called
for his gun. I leaned mine against a hollow withy
pollard, and called 'ready.'

Taking his gun a few inches above the trigger
guard (and with the guard towards his side), holding
it lightly just where it seemed to balance in a perpendicular position, I gave it a slow heave rather than a
throw, and it rose into the air. This peculiar *feeling*

hoist, as it were, caused it to retain the perpendicular position as it passed over brook and hedge in a low curve. As it descended it did indeed slope a little, and Orion caught it with one hand easily. The hedge being low he could see it coming ; but guns are sometimes heaved in this way over hedges that have not been cropped for years. Then the gun suddenly appears in the air, perhaps fifteen feet high, while the catch depends not only upon the dexterity of the hand but the ear—to judge correctly where the person who throws it is standing, as he is invisible.

The spaniels plunged in the brook among the flags, but though they made a great splashing nothing came of it till we approached a marshy place where was a pond. A moorhen then rose and scuttled down the brook, her legs dragging along the surface some distance before she could get up, and the sunshine sparkling on the water that dropped from her. I fired and knocked her over : at the sound of the discharge a bird rose from the low mound by the pond some forty yards ahead. My second barrel was empty in an instant.

Both Orion's followed ; but the distance, the intervening pollard willows, or our excitement spoilt the aim. The woodcock flew off untouched, and

made straight away from the territories we could
beat into those that. were jealously guarded by a
certain keeper with whom Farmer 'Willum' had
waged war for years.   'Come on!' shouted Orion as
soon as he had marked the cock down in a mound
two fields away.   Throwing him my gun, I leaped
the brook ; and we at first raced, but on second
thoughts walked slowly, for the mound.   Running
disturbs accuracy of fire, and a woodcock was much
too rare a visitor for the slightest chance to be lost.

As we approached we considered that very probably the cock would either lie close till we had
walked past, and get up behind, or he would rise out
of gunshot.   What we were afraid of was his making
for the preserves, which were not far off.   So we
tossed for the best position, and I lost.   I had therefore to get over on the side of the hedge towards the
preserves and to walk down somewhat faster than
Orion, who was to keep (on his side) about thirty
yards behind.   The object was to flush the cock on
his side, so that if missed the bird might return
towards our territories.   In a double-mound like this
it is impossible to tell what a woodcock will do, but
this was the best thing we could think of.

About half-way down the hedge I heard Orion
fire both barrels in quick succession—the mound was

so thick I could not see through. The next instant the cock came over the top of the hedge just above my head. Startled at seeing me so close, he flew straight down along the summit of the bushes—a splendid chance to look at from a distance; but in throwing up the gun a projecting briar caught the barrels, and before I could recover it the bird came down at the side of the hedge.

It was another magnificent chance; but again three pollard willows interfered, and as I fired the bark flew off one of them in small strips. Quickened by the whistling pellets, the cock suddenly lifted himself again to the top of the hedge to go over, and for a moment came full in view, and quite fifty yards away. I fired a snap shot as a forlorn hope, and lost sight of him; but the next instant I heard Orion call, 'He's down!' One single chance pellet had dropped the cock—he fell on the other side just under the hedge.

We hastened back to the brook, thinking that the shooting would attract the keepers, and did not stay to look at the bird till safe over the water. The long beak, the plumage that seems painted almost in the exact tints of the dead brown leaves he loves so well, the eyes large by comparison and so curiously placed towards the poll of the head as if to see behind him

—there was not a point that did not receive its share of admiration. We shot about half a dozen rabbits, two more hares, and a woodpigeon afterwards; but all these were nothing compared with the woodcock.

How Farmer 'Willum' chuckled over it—especially to think that we had cut out the game from the very batteries of the enemy! It was the one speck of bitterness in the old man's character—his hatred of this keeper. Disabled himself by age and rheumatism from walking far, he heard daily reports from his men of this fellow coming over the boundary to shoot, or drive pheasant or partridge away. It was a sight to see Farmer 'Willum' stretch his bulky length in his old armchair, right before the middle of the great fire of logs on the hearth, twiddling his huge thumbs, and every now and then indulging in a hearty laugh, followed by a sip at the 'straight-cup.'

There was a stag's horn over the staircase : 'Willum' loved to tell how it came there. One severe winter long since, the deer in the forest many miles away broke cover, forced by hunger, and came into the rickyards and even the gardens. Most of them were got back, but one or two wandered beyond trace. Those who had guns were naturally on the look-out; indeed, a regular hunt was got up— 'Willum,' then young and active, in it of course. This chase was not successful ; but early one morning, going to look for wild geese in the water-meadow with his long-barrelled gun, he saw something in a lonely rickyard. Creeping cautiously up, he rested the heavy gun on an ash stole, and the big duck-shot tore its way into the stag's shoulder. Those days were gone, but still his interest in shooting was unabated.

Nothing had been altered on the place since he was a boy : the rent even was the same. But all that is now changed—swept away before modern improvements ; and the rare old man is gone too, and I think his only enemy also.

There was nothing I used to look forward to, as the summer waned, with so much delight as the snipe shooting. Regularly as the swallow to the eaves in spring, the snipe comes back with the early frosts of autumn to the same well-known spots—to the bend of the brook or the boggy corner in the ploughed field— but in most uncertain numbers. Sometimes flocks of ten or twenty, sometimes only twos and threes are seen, but always haunting particular places.

They have a special affection for peaty ground, black and spongy, where every footstep seems to squeeze water out of the soil with a slight hissing sound, and the boot cuts through the soft turf. There, where a slow stream winds in and out, unmarked by willow or bush, but fringed with green aquatic grasses growing on a margin of ooze, the snipe finds tempting food ; or in the meadows where a little spring breaks forth in the ditch and does not freeze—for water which has just bubbled out of the earth possesses this peculiarity, and is therefore favourable to low forms of insect or slug life in winter—the snipe may be found when the ponds are bound with ice.

Some of the old country folk used to make as much mystery about this bird as the cuckoo. Because it was seldom seen till the first fogs the belief was that it had lost its way in the mist at sea, and come inland by mistake.

Just as in the early part of the year green buds and opening flowers welcome swallow and cuckoo, so the colours of the dying leaf prepare the way for the second feathered immigration in autumn. Once now and then the tints of autumn are so beautiful that the artist can hardly convey what he sees to canvas. The maples are aglow with orange, the oaks one mass of buff, the limes light gold, the elms a soft yellow. In the hawthorn thickets bronze spots abound ; here and there a bramble leaf has turned a brilliant crimson (though many bramble leaves will remain a dull green all the winter through) ; the edible chestnut sheds leaves of a dark fawn hue, but all, scattered by the winds, presently resolve into a black pulp upon the earth. Noting these signs the sportsman gets out his dust-shot for the snipe, and the farmer, as he sees the fieldfare flying over after a voyage from Norway, congratulates himself that last month was reasonably dry, and enabled him to sow his winter seed.

' Sceap—sceap !' and very often the snipe successfully carries out the intention expressed in his odd-sounding cry, and does escape in reality. Although I could not at first put my theory into practice, yet I found by experience that it was correct. He is the exception to the golden rule that the safest way lies in the middle, and that therefore you should fire not too soon nor too late, but half-way between. But the snipe must either be knocked over the instant he rises from the ground, and before he has time to commence his puzzling zig-zag flight, or else you must wait till he has finished his corkscrew burst.

Then there is a moment just before he passes out of range when he glides in a straight line and may be hit. This singular zig-zag flight so deceives the eye as almost to produce the idea of a spiral movement. No barrel can ever be jerked from side to side swiftly enough, no hair-trigger is fine enough, to catch him then, except by the chance of a vast scattering overcharge, which has nothing to do with sport. If he rises at some little distance, then fire instantly, because by the time the zig-zag is done the range will be too great; if he starts up under your feet, out of a bunch of rushes, as is often the case, then give him law till his eccentric twist is finished.

When the smoke has cleared away in the crisp air, there he lies, the yet warm breast on the frozen ground, to be lifted up not without a passing pity and admiration. The brown feathers are exquisitely shaded, and so exactly resemble the hue of the rough dead aquatic grass out of which he sprang that if you cast the bird among it you will have some trouble to find it again. To discover a living snipe on the ground is indeed a test of good eyesight; for as he slips in and out among the brown withered flags and the grey grass it requires not only a quick eye but the in-bred sportsman's instinct of perception (if such a phrase is permissible) to mark him out.

If your shot has missed and merely splashed up the water or rattled against bare branches, then step swiftly behind a tree-trunk, and stay in ambuscade, keeping a sharp watch on him as he circles round high up in the air. Very often in a few minutes he will come back in a wide sweep, and drop scarcely a gun-shot distant in the same watercourse, when a second shot may be obtained. The little jack snipe, when flushed, will never fly far, if shot at several times in succession, still settling fifty or sixty yards farther on, and is easily bagged.

Coming silently as possible round a corner, treading gently on the grass still white with hoar-frost in the shadow of the bushes, you may chance to spring a stray woodcock, which bird, if you lose a moment, will put the hedge between him and you. Artists used to seek for certain feathers which he carries, one in each wing, thinking to make of them a more delicate brush than the finest camel's hair.

In the evening I used to hide in the osier-beds on the edge of a great water-meadow ; for now that the marshes are drained, and the black earth of the fens yields a harvest of yellow corn, the broad level meads which are irrigated to fertilise them are among the chief inland resorts of wild fowl. When the bright moon is rising, you walk in among the tapering osier-wands, the rustling sedges, and dead dry hemlock stems, and wait behind an aspen tree.

In the thick blackthorn bush a round dark ball indicates the blackbird, who has puffed out his feathers to shield him from the frost, and who will sit so close and quiet that you may see the moonlight glitter on his eye. Presently comes a whistling noise of wings, and a loud 'quack, quack!' as a string of ducks, their long necks stretched out, pass over not twenty yards high, slowly slanting downwards to the water. This is the favourable moment for the gun, because their big bodies are well defined against the sky, and aim can be taken ; but to shoot anything on the ground at night, even a rabbit, whose white tail as he hops away is fairly visible, is most difficult.

The baffling shadows and the moonbeams on the barrel, and the faint reflection from the dew or hoar frost on the grass, prevent more than a general direction being given to the gun, even with the tiny piece of white paper which some affix to the muzzle-sight as a guide. From a punt with a swivel gun it is different, because the game is swimming and visible as black dots on the surface, and half a pound of shot is sure to hit something. But in the water-meadows the ducks get among the grass, and the larger water carriers where they can swim usually have small raised banks, so that at a distance only the heads of the birds appear above them.

So that the best time to shoot a duck is just as he slopes down to settle—first, because he is distinctly visible against the sky ; next, because he is within easy range ; and, lastly, his flight is steady. If you attempt to have ducks driven towards you though they may go right overhead, yet it will often be too high—for they rise at a sharp angle when frightened ; and men who are excellent judges of distance when it is a hare running across the fallow, find themselves all at fault trying to shoot at any elevation. Perhaps this arises from the peculiarity of the human eye which draughtsmen are fond of illustrating by asking a tyro to correctly bisect a vertical line : a thing that looks easy, and is really only to be done by long practice.

To make certain of selecting the right spot in the osiers over which the ducks will pass, for one or two evenings previously a look-out should be kept and their usual course observed ; for all birds and animals, even the wildest wild fowl, are creatures of habit and custom, and having once followed a particular path will continue to use it until seriously disturbed. Evening after evening the ducks will rise above the horizon at the same place and almost at the same time, and fly straight to their favourite feeding-place.

If hit, the mallard falls with a thud on the earth, for he is a heavy bird ; and few are more worthy of powder and shot either for his savoury flavour, far surpassing the tame duck, or the beauty of his burnished neck. With the ducks come teal and widgeon and moorhen, till the swampy meadow resounds with their strange cries. When ponds and lakes are frozen hard is the best time for sport in these irrigated fields. All day long the ducks will stand or waddle to and fro on the ice in the centre of the lake or mere, far out of reach and ready to rise at the slightest alarm. But at night they seek the meadow where the water, running swiftly in the carriers, never entirely freezes, and where, if the shallow spots become ice, the rising current flows over it and floods another place.

There is, moreover, never any difficulty in getting the game when hit, because the water, except in the main carriers, which you can leap across, hardly rises to the ankle, and ordinary water-tight boots will enable you to wade wherever necessary. This is a great advantage with wild fowl, which are sometimes shot and lost in deep ooze and strong currents and eddies, and on thin ice where men cannot go and even good dogs are puzzled.

CHAPTER XI

FERRETING: A RABBIT-HUNTER

THE ferreting season commences when the frosts have caused the leaves to drop, and the rabbits grow fat from feeding on bark. Early one December morning, Orion and I started, with our man Little John, to ferret a double-mound for our old friend Farmer 'Willum' at Redcote.

Little John was a labourer—one of those frequently working at odd times for Luke, the Rabbit-Contractor. We had nicknamed him Little John because of his great size and unwieldy proportions. He was the most useful man we knew for such work; his heart was so thoroughly in it.

He was waiting for us before we had finished breakfast, with his tools and implements, having carefully prepared these while yet it was dark at home in his cottage. The nets require looking to before starting, as they are apt to get into a tangle, and there is nothing so annoying as to have to unravel strings with chilled fingers in a ditch. Some have to be mended, having been torn ; some are cast aside altogether because weak and rotten. The twine having been frequently saturated with water has decayed. All the nets are of a light yellow colour from the clay and sand that has worked into the string.

These nets almost filled a sack, into which he also cast a pair of 'owl-catchers,' gloves of stout white leather, thick enough to turn a thorn while handling bushes, or to withstand the claws of an owl furiously resisting capture. His ferrets cost him much thought which to take and which to leave behind. He had also to be particular how he fed them—they must be eager for prey, and yet they must not be starved, else they would gorge on the blood of the first rabbit, and become useless for hunting.

Two had to be muzzled—an operation of some difficulty that generally results in a scratched hand. A small piece of small but strong twine is passed through the jaws behind the tusk-like teeth, and tightly tied round, so tightly as almost to cut into the skin. This is the old way of muzzling a ferret, handed down from generations : Little John scorns the muzzles that can be bought at shops, and still more despises the tiny bells to hang round the neck.

The first he says often come off, and the second embarrass the ferret and sometimes catch in projecting rootlets and hold it fast. He has, too, a line—many yards of stout twine wound about a short stick—to line a ferret if necessary.

The ferrets are placed in a smaller bag, tightly tied at the top—for they will work through and get out if any aperture be left. Inside the bag is a little hay for them to lay on. He prefers the fitchew ferret as he calls it; that is the sort that are coloured like a polecat. He says they are fiercer, larger of make and more powerful. But he has also a couple of white ones with pink eyes. Besides the sack of nets, the bag of ferrets, and a small bundle in a knotted handkerchief—his 'nuncheon'—which in themselves make a tolerable load, he has brought a billhook, and a 'navigator,' or draining-tool.

This is a narrow spade of specially stout make; the blade is hollow and resembles an exaggerated gouge, and the advantage is that in digging out a rabbit the tool is very apt to catch under a root, when an ordinary spade may bend and become useless. The 'navigator' will stand anything, and being narrow is also more handy. All these implements Little John has prepared by the dim light of a horn lantern in the shed at the back of his cottage. A mug of ale while we get our guns greatly cheers him, and unlooses his tongue.

All the way to Redcote he impresses on us the absolute necessity for silence while ferreting, and congratulates us on having a nearly still day. He is a little doubtful about Orion's spaniel and whether it will keep quiet or not.

When we reach the double-mound, his talk entirely ceases : he is as silent and as rugged as a pollard oak. By the top of the mound the sack of nets is thrown down on the sward and opened. As there are more holes on the other side of the hedge Orion goes over with Little John, and I proceed to set up the nets on mine.

I found some difficulty in getting at the bank, the bushes being so thick, and had to use the billhook and chop a way in : I heard Little John growling about this in a whisper to Orion. Very often before going with the ferrets people send a man or two a few hours previously to chop and clear the bushes. The effect is that the rabbits will not bolt freely. They hear the men chopping, and the vibration of the earth as they clumsily climb over the banks, and will not come out till absolutely forced. If it is done at all, it should be done a week beforehand. This was why Little

John grumbled at my chopping though he knew it was necessary.

To set up a rabbit net you must arrange it so that it covers the whole of the mouth of the hole, for if there is any opening between it and the bank the rabbit will slip through. He will not face the net unless obliged to. Along the upper part, if the bank is steep, so that the net will not lie on it of itself, two or three little twigs should be thrust through the meshes into the earth to suspend it.

These twigs should be no larger than are used by birds in constructing their nests ; just strong enough to hold the net in place and no more. On the other hand, care must be taken that no stout projecting root catches a corner of the net, else it will not draw up properly and the rabbit will escape.

Little John, not satisfied with my assurance that I had netted all the holes my side, now came over—crawling on hands and knees that he might not jar the bank—to examine for himself. His practised eye detected two holes that I had missed : one on the top of the mound much overhung by dead grass, and one under a stole. These he attended to. He then crawled up on the mound two or three yards below the end of the bury, and with his own hands stretched a larger net right across the top of the bank, so that if a rabbit did escape he would run into this. To be still more sure he stretched another similar net across the whole width of the mound at the other end of the bury.

He then undid the mouth of the ferret bag, holding it between his knees—the ferrets immediately attempted to struggle out: he selected two and then tied it up again. With both these in his own hands, for he would trust nothing to another, he slipped quietly back to Orion's side, and so soon as he saw I was standing well back placed them in different holes.

Almost the next instant one came out my side disarranging a net. I got into the ditch, hastily reset the net, and put the ferret to an adjacent hole, lifting up the corner of the net there for it to creep in. Unlike the weasel, a ferret once outside a hole seems at a loss, and wanders slowly about, till chance brings him to a second. The weasel used to hunting is no sooner out of one hole than he darts away to the next. But this power the ferret has partially lost from confinement.

For a moment the ferret hesitated inside the hole, as if undecided which of two passages to take: then he started, and I lost sight of his tail. Hardly had I

got back to my stand than I heard Little John leap
into the ditch his side: the next minute I saw the
body of the rabbit which he had killed thrown out
into the field.

I stood behind a somewhat advanced bush that
came out into the meadow like a buttress, and kept
an eye on the holes along the bank. It is essential to
stand well back from the holes and, if possible, out of
sight. In a few moments something moved, and I
saw the head of a rabbit at the mouth of a hole just
behind the net. He looked through the meshes as
through a lattice, and I could see his nostrils work, as
he considered within himself how to pass this thing.
It was but for a moment; the ferret came behind,
and wild with hereditary fear, the rabbit leaped into
the net.

The force of the spring not only drew the net
together, but dragged out the peg, and rabbit and net
inextricably entangled rolled down the bank to the
bottom of the ditch. I jumped into the ditch and
seized the net; when there came a hoarse whisper:
'Look sharp you, mcaster: put up another net fust—
he can't get out; hould un under your arm, *or in your
teeth.*'

I looked up, and saw Little John's face peering
over the mound. He had thrust himself up under

the bushes; his hat was off; his weather-beaten face bleeding from a briar, but he could not feel the scratch so anxious was he that nothing should escape. I pulled another net from my pocket, and spread it roughly over the hole; then more slowly took the rabbit from the other net.

You should never hold a rabbit up till you have got fast hold of his hind legs; he will so twist and work himself as to get free from any other grasp. But when held by the hind legs and lifted from the ground he can do nothing. I now returned to my buttress of bushes and waited. The rabbits did not bolt my side again for awhile. Every now and then I saw, or heard, Orion or Little John leap into their ditch, and well knew what it meant before the dead rabbit was cast out to fall with a helpless thud upon the sward.

Once I saw a rabbit's head at the mouth of a hole, and momentarily expected him to dart forth driven by the same panic fear. But either the ferret passed, or there was another side-tunnel—the rabbit went back. Some few minutes afterwards Little John exclaimed: 'Look out, you: ferret's out!' One of the ferrets had come out of a hole and was aimlessly—as it appeared—roaming along the bank.

As he came nearest my side, I got quietly into the

ditch and seized him, and put him into a hole. To
my surprise he refused to go in—I pushed him : he
returned and continued to try to come out till I gave
him a sharp fillip with the finger, when he shook the
dust and particles of dry earth from his fur with a
shiver, as if in protest, and slowly disappeared inside
the hole.

As I was creeping out of the deep ditch on hands
and knees, I heard Orion call angrily to the spaniel to
come to heel. Hitherto the spaniel had sat on his
haunches behind Orion fairly quiet and still, though not
without an occasional restless movement. But now
he broke suddenly from all control, and disregarding
Orion's anger—though with hanging tail—rushed into
the hedge, and along the top of the mound where there
was a thick mass of dead grass. Little John hurled
a clod of clay at him, but before I was quite out of
the ditch the spaniel gave tongue, and at the same
moment I saw a rabbit come from the ditch and run
like mad across the field.

The dog gave chase—I rushed for my gun, which
was some yards off, placed against a hollow withy
tree. The haste disconcerted the aim—the rabbit too
was almost fifty yards away when I fired. But the
shot broke one hind leg—it trailed behind—and the
spaniel had him instantly. 'Look at yer nets,' said

Little John in a tone of suppressed indignation, for he disliked the noise of a gun, as all other noises.

I did look, and found that one net had been partly pushed aside : yet to so small an extent that I should hardly have believed it possible for the rabbit to have crept through. He must have slipped out without the slightest sound and quietly got on the top of the mound without being seen. But there, alas ! he found a wide net stretched right across the bank so that to slip down the mound on the top was impossible. That would certainly have been his course had not the net been there.

It was now doubtless that the spaniel caught wind of him, and the scent was so strong that it overcame his obedience. The moment the dog got on the bank, the rabbit slipped down into the rushes in the ditch —I did not see him because my back was turned in the act to scramble out. Then, directly the spaniel gave tongue the rabbit darted for the open, hoping to reach the buries in the hedge on the opposite side of the meadow.

This incident explained why the ferret seemed so loth to go back into the hole. He had crept out some few moments behind the rabbit and in his aimless uncertain manner was trying to follow the scent along the bank. He did not like being compelled to

give up this scent and to search again for another.
'Us must be main careful how us fixes our nets, you,'
said Little John, going as far as he could in reproof of
my negligence.

The noise of the gun, the barking, and talking
was of course heard by the rabbits still in the bury,
and as if to show that Little John was right, for a while
they ceased to bolt. Standing behind the bushes—
against which I now placed the gun to be nearer at
hand—I watched the nets till my eye was caught by
the motions of the ferret bag. It lay on the grass
and had hitherto been inert. But now the bag reared
itself up, and then rolled over, to again rise and again
tumble. The ferrets left in it in reserve were eager
to get out—sharp set on account of a scanty breakfast
—and their motions caused the bag to roll along a
short distance.

I could see Orion on the other side of the mound
tolerably well because he was standing up and the
leaves had fallen from the upper part of the bushes.
Little John was crouched in the ditch : the dead
grasses, 'gicks,' withered vines of bryony, the thistles,
and dark shrivelled fern concealed him.

There was a round black sloe on the blackthorn
beside me, the beautiful gloss, or bloom, on it made it
look like a tiny plum. It tasted not only sour, but

seemed to positively fill the mouth with a rough acid. Overhead light grey clouds, closely packed but not rainy, drifted very slowly before a N.E. upper current. Occasionally a brief puff of wind came through the bushes rustling the dead leaves that still remained on the oaks.

Despite the cold, something of Little John's intense concentration communicated itself to us: we waited and watched with eager patience. After a while he got out of the ditch where he had been listening with his ear close against the bank, and asked me to pass him the ferret-bag. He took out another ferret and lined it—that is, attached one end of a long string to its neck, and then sent it in.

He watched which way the ferret turned, and then again placed his head upon the hard clay to listen. Orion had to come and hold the line, while he went two or three yards farther down, got into the ditch and once more listened carefully. 'He be about the middle of the mound you,' he said to me ; 'he be between you and I. Lor! look out.'

There was a low rumbling sound—I expected to see a rabbit bolt into one of my nets. I heard Little John moving some leaves, and then he shouted, 'Give I a net, you—quick. Lor! here be another hole : he's coming !' I looked over the mound and saw Little

John, his teeth set and staring at a hole which had no net, his great hands open ready to pounce instantly like some wild animal on its prey. In an instant the rabbit bolted—he clutched it and clasped it tight to his chest. There was a moment of struggling, the next the rabbit was held up for a moment and then cast across his knee.

It was always a sight to see Little John's keen delight in 'wristing' their necks. He affected utter unconsciousness of what he was doing, looked you in the face, and spoke about some indifferent subject. But all the while he was feeling the rabbit's muscles stretch before the terrible grasp of his hands, and an expression of complacent satisfaction flitted over his features as the neck gave with a sudden looseness, and in a moment what had been a living straining creature became limp.

The ferret came out after the rabbit; he immediately caught it and thrust it into his pocket. There were still two ferrets in—one that was suspected to be gorging on a rabbit in a *cul de sac*, and the other lined, and which had gone to join that sanguinary feast. The use of the line was to trace where the loose ferret lay. 'Chuck I the show'l, measter,' said Little John.

I gave the 'navigator' tool a heave over the hedge; it fell and stuck upright in the sward. Orion handed it to him. He first filled up the hole from which a rabbit had just bolted with a couple of 'spits,' *i.e.* spadefuls, and then began to dig on the top of the mound.

This digging was very tedious. The roots of the thorn bushes and trees constantly impeded it, and had to be cut. Then upon at last getting down to the hole, it was found that the right place had not been hit by several feet. Here was the line and the lined ferret— he had got hitched in a projecting root, and was furiously struggling to go forward to the feast of blood.

Another spell of digging—this time still slower because Little John was afraid lest the edge of his tool should suddenly slip through and cut his ferret on the head, and perhaps kill it. At last the place was reached and the ferret drawn forth still clinging to its victim. The rabbit was almost beyond recognition as a rabbit. The poor creature had been stopped by a *cul de sac*, and the ferret came upon him from behind.

As the hole was small the rabbit's body completely filled it, and the ferret could not scramble past to get at the spot behind the ear where it usually seizes. The ferret had therefore deliberately gnawn away the hind-quarters and so bored a passage. The ferret being so gorged was useless for further hunting and was replaced in the bag. But Little John gave him a drink of water first from the bottom of the ditch.

Orion and I, wearied with the digging, now insisted on removing to the next bury, for we felt sure that the remaining rabbits in this one would not bolt. Little John had no choice but to comply, but he did so with much reluctance and many rueful glances back at the holes from which he took the nets. He was sure, he said, that there were at least half-a-dozen still in the bury: he only wished he might have all that he could get out of it. But we imperiously ordered a removal.

We went some thirty yards down the mound, passing many smaller buries, and chose a spot perfectly drilled with holes. While Little John was in the ditch putting up nets, we slily undid the ferret bag and turned three ferrets at once loose into the holes. 'Lor! measter, measter, what be you at?' cried Little John, quite beside himself. 'You'll spoil all on it. Lor!'

A sharp report as Orion fired at a rabbit that bolted almost under Little John's fingers drowned his remonstrances, and he had to scramble out of the way quick. Bang! bang! right and left: the firing became rapid. There being no nets to alarm the rabbits and three ferrets hunting them, they tumbled out in all directions as fast as we could load. Now the cartridges struck branches and shattered them. Now the shot flattened itself against sarsen stones imbedded in the mound. The rabbits had scarce a yard to bolt from one hole to another, so that it was sharp work.

Little John now gave up all hope, and only pleaded piteously for his ferrets. ' Mind as you doan't hit 'em, measter ; doant'ee shoot into a hole, you.' For half an hour we had some really good shooting : then it began to slacken, and we told him to catch his ferrets and go on to the next bury. I am not sure that he would not have rebelled outright but just then a boy came up carrying a basket of provisions, and a large earthenware jar with a bung cork, full of humming ale. Farmer Willum had sent this, and the strong liquor quite restored Little John's good humour. It really was ale—such as is not to be got for money.

The boy said that he had seen Farmer Willum's hereditary enemy, the keeper, watching us from his side of the boundary, doubtless attracted by the sound of the firing. He said also that there was a pheasant in a little copse beside the brook. We sent him out again to reconnoitre : he returned and repeated that the keeper had gone, and that he thought he saw him enter the distant fir plantations.

So we left the boy to help Little John at the next bury—a commission that made him grin with delight, and suited the other very well, since the noisy guns were going away, and he could use his nets.

We took the lined ferret with us, and started after the pheasant. Just as we approached the copse, the spaniel gave tongue on the other side of the hedge. Orion had tied him up to a bush, wishing to leave him with Little John. But the spaniel tore and twisted till he got loose and had followed us—keeping out of sight—till now crossing the scent of a rabbit he set up his bark. We called him to heel, and I am afraid he got a kick. But the pheasant was alarmed and rose before we could properly enfilade the little copse, where we should most certainly have had him. He flew high and straight for the fir plantations, where it was useless to follow.

However, we leaped the brook and entered the keeper's territory under shelter of a thick double-mound. We slipped the lined ferret into a small bury, and succeeded in knocking over a couple of rabbits. The object of using the lined ferret was because we could easily recover it. This was pure mischief, for there were scores of rabbits on our own side. But then there was just a little spice of risk in this, and we knew Willum would gloat over it.

After firing these two shots we got back again as speedily as possible, and once more assisted Little John. We could not, however, quite resist the pleasure of shooting a rabbit occasionally and so tormenting him. We left one hole each side without a net, and insisted on the removal of the net that stretched across the top of the bank. This gave us a shot now and then, and the removal of the cross net allowed the rabbit some little law.

Notwithstanding these drawbacks — to him — Little John succeeded in making a good bag. He stayed till it was quite dark to dig out a ferret that had killed a rabbit in the hole. He took his money for his day's work with indifference : but when we presented him with two couple of clean rabbits his gratitude was too much for him to express. The gnawn and ' blown ' rabbits [by shot] were his per-quisite, the clean rabbits an unexpected gift. It was not their monetary value ; it was the fact that they were rabbits.

The man's instinct for hunting was so strong that it seemed to overcome everything else. He would walk miles—after a long day's farm work—just to help old Luke, the rabbit contractor, bring home the rabbits in the evening from the Upper Woods. He worked regularly for one farmer, and did his work well : he was a sober man too as men go, that is he did not get drunk more than once a month.   A strong man must drink now and then : but he was not a sot, and took nine-tenths of his money faithfully home to his wife and children.

In the winter when farm work is not so pressing he was allowed a week off now and then, which he spent in ferreting for the farmers, and sometimes for Luke, and of course he was only too glad to get such an engagement as we gave him.   Sometimes he made a good thing of his ferreting : sometimes when the weather was bad it was a failure.   But although a few shillings were of consequence to him, it really did not seem to be the money-value but the sport that he loved.   To him that sport was all-absorbing.

His ferrets were well looked after, and he some- times sold one for a good price to keepers.   As a rule a man who keeps ferrets is suspected : but Little John was too well understood, and he had no difficulty in begging a little milk for them.

His tenacity in pursuit of a rabbit was always a source of wonder to me.   In rain, in wind, in frost ; his feet up to the ankle in the ice-cold slush at the bottom of a ditch : no matter what the weather or how rough, he patiently stood to his nets.   I have known him stand the whole day long in a snowstorm

—the snow on the ground and in the holes, the flakes drifting against his face—and never once show impatience.   All he disliked was wind—not on account of discomfort, but because the creaking of the branches and the howling of the blast made such a noise that it was impossible to tell where the rabbit would bolt.

He congratulated himself that evening because he had recovered all his ferrets.   Sometimes one will lie in and defy all efforts to bring it out.   One plan is to place a dead fresh rabbit at the mouth of the hole which may tempt the ferret to come and seize it.   In large woods there are generally one or more ferrets wandering loose in the season, that have escaped from the keepers or poachers.

If the keeper sees one he tries to catch it, failing that he puts a charge of shot into it.   Some keepers think nothing of shooting their own ferrets if they will not come when called by the chirrup with the lips, or displease them in other ways.   They do not care, because they can have as many as they like. Little John made pets of his: they obeyed him very well as a rule.

Poaching men are sometimes charged with stealing ferrets, *i.e.* with picking up and carrying off those

that keepers have lost. A ferret is, however, a difficult thing to identify and swear to.

Those who go poaching with ferrets choose a
moonlight night: if it is dark it is difficult to find the
holes. Small buries are best because so much more
easily managed, and the ferret is usually lined. If a
large bury is attempted, they take the first half-dozen
that bolt and then move on to another. The first
rabbits come out rapidly; the rest linger as if warned
by the fate of their companions. Instead of wasting
time over them it is best to move to another place.

Unless a keeper should chance to pass up the
hedgerow there is comparatively little risk, for the
men are in the ditch and invisible ten yards away
under the bushes and make no noise. It is more
difficult to get home with the game: but it is managed.
Very small buries with not more than four or five
holes may be ferreted even on the darkest nights by
carefully observing beforehand where the holes are
situate.

CHAPTER XII

A WINTER NIGHT: OLD TRICKS: PHEASANT-STALK-
  ING: MATCHLOCK *VERSUS* BREECHLOADER:
  CONCLUSION

WHEN the moon is full and nearly at the zenith it
seems to move so slowly that the shadows scarcely
change their position.   In winter, when the branches
are bare, a light that is nearly vertical over a tree
can cast but little shadow, and that falls immediately
around the trunk.   So that the smallness of the
shadow itself and the slowness of its motion together
tend to conceal it.

The snow on the ground increases the sense of
light, and in approaching the wood the scene is even
more distinct than during the gloomy day.   The tips
of the short stubble that has not yet been ploughed
in places just protrude above the surface, and the
snow, frozen hard, crunches with a low sound under
foot.   But for that all is perfectly still.   The level
upland cornfields stretch away white and vacant to

the hills—white, too, and clear against the sky. The plain is silent, and nothing that can be seen moves upon its surface.

On the verge of the wood which occupies the sloping ground there stands a great oak tree, and down one side of its trunk is a narrow white streak of snow. Leaning against the oak and looking upwards, every branch and twig is visible, lit up by the moon. Overhead the stars are dimmed, but they shine more brightly yonder above the hills. Such leaves as have not yet fallen hang motionless: those that are lying on the ground are covered by the snow, and thus held fast from rustling even were the wind to blow. But there is not the least breath—a great frost is always quiet, profoundly quiet—and the silence is undisturbed even by the fall of a leaf. The frost that kills them holds the leaves till it melts, and then they drop.

The tall ash poles behind in the wood stand stark and straight, pointing upwards, and it is possible to see for some distance between them. No lesser bats flit to and fro outside the fence under the branches; no larger ones pass above the tops of the trees. There seems, indeed, a total absence of life. The pheasants are at roost in the warmer covers; and the woodpigeons are also perched—some in the detached oaks of the hedgerows, particularly those that are thickly grown with ivy about the upper branches.   Up in the great beeches the rooks are still and silent ; sometimes the boughs are encrusted with rime about their very claws.

Leaving the oak now and skirting the wood, after a while the meadows on the lower ground are reached ; and here perhaps the slight scampering sound of a rabbit may be heard.   But as they can see and hear you so far in the bright light and silence, they will most likely be gone before you can get near.   They are restless—very restless ; first because of the snow, and next because of the moonlight.   The hares, unable to find anything on the hills or the level white plain above, have come down here and search along the sheltered hedgerows for leaf and blade.   To-night the rabbits will run almost like the hares, to and fro, hither and thither.

In the thickest hawthorns the blackbirds and lesser feathered creatures are roosting, preferring the hedgerow to the more open wood.   Some of the lesser birds have crept into the ivy around the elms, and which crowns the tops of the withy pollards. Wrens and sparrows have gone to the hayricks, roosting in little holes in the sides under the slightly projecting thatch.   They have taken refuge too in the nest-holes made in the thatched eaves of the sheds : tits are there also ; and sometimes two or three of the latter are captured at once in such holes.

A dark line across the lower meadows marks the course of the brook ; it is dark because the snow falling on the water melted. Even now there is a narrow stream unfrozen ; though the banks against which it chafes are hard, and will not take the impression of the moorhen's foot. The water-rats that in summer-time played and fed along the margin among the flags are rarely seen in winter. In walking in daylight by the brook now their plunge into the water will not be heard, nor can they be seen travelling at the bottom.

They lay up a store of food in a hole away from the stream, generally choosing the banks or higher ground in the withy-beds—places that are not often flooded. Their ordinary holes, which are half, and sometimes quite, under water, will not do for winter ; they would be frozen in them, and perhaps their store of food would be spoiled ; besides which the floods cause the stream to rise above its banks, and they could not exist under water for weeks together.

Sill further down, where the wood ends in scattered bushes and withy-beds, the level shore of the shallow mere succeeds. The once soft, oozy ground is now firm ; the rushes are frozen stiff, and the ice for some distance out is darkened by the aquatic weeds frozen in it. From here the wood, rising up the slope, comes into view at once—the dark trees, the ash poles, the distant beeches, the white crest of the hill—all still and calm under the moonlight. The level white plain of ice behind stretches away, its real extent concealed by the islands of withy and the dark pines along the distant shore ; while elsewhere the ice is not distinguishable from the almost equally level fields that join it. Looking now more closely on the snow, the tracks of hares and rabbits that have crossed and recrossed the ice are visible.

In passing close to the withy-beds to return to the wood some branches have to be pushed aside and cause a slight noise. Immediately a crowd of birds rise out of the withies, where they have been roosting, and scatter into the night. They are redwings and thrushes ; every withy-bed is full of them. After wheeling about in the air they will presently return— first one, then three or four, and finally the flock, to their roosting-place.

It is easy now to walk through the wood without making a noise : there is room to pass between the stoles of ash ; and the dead sticks that would have cracked under foot are covered with snow. But be careful how you step ; for in some places the snow has fallen upon a mass of leaves filling a swampy hollow. Above there is a thin crust of snow, but under the leaves the oozy ground is still soft.

Upon the dark pines the snow has lodged, making the boughs bend downwards. Where the slope becomes a hill the ash stoles and nut-tree bushes are far apart and thinner, so that there are wide white spaces around them. Regaining now the top of the hill where the plain comes to the verge of the wood, there is a clear view down across the ash poles to the withies, the white mere, and the meadows below. Everywhere silence, stillness, sleep.

In the high trees slumbering creatures ; in the hedgerows, in the bushes, and the withies birds with feathers puffed out, slumbering ; in the banks, under the very ground, dormant animals. A quiet cold that at first does not seem cold because it is so quiet, but which gradually seizes on and stills the sap of plants and the blood of living things. A ruthless frost, still, subtle, and irresistible, that will slay the bird on its perch and weaken the swift hare.

The most cruel of all things this snow and frost, because of the torture of hunger which the birds must feel even in their sleep. But how beautiful the round full moon, the brilliant light, the white landscape, the graceful lines of the pine brought out by the snow, the hills yonder, and the stars rising above them !

It was on just such a night as this that some years since a most successful raid was made upon this wood by a band of poachers coming from a distance. The pheasants had been kept later than usual to be shot by a Christmas party, and perhaps this had caused a relaxation of vigilance. The band came in a cart of some kind ; the marks of the wheels were found on the snow where it had been driven off the highway and across a field to some ricks. There, no doubt, the horse and cart were kept out of sight behind the ricks, while the men, who were believed to have worn smock-frocks, entered the wood.

The bright moonlight made it easy to find the pheasants, and they were potted in plenty. Finding that there was no opposition, the gang crossed from the wood to some outlying plantations and continued their work there. The keeper never heard a sound. He was an old man—a man who had been on the estate all his life—and had come in late in the evening after a long round. He sat by the fire of split logs and enjoyed the warmth after the bitter cold and frost ; and as he himself confessed, took an extra glass in consideration of the severity of the weather.

His wife was old and deaf. Neither of them heard

the guns nor the dogs. Those in the kennels close
to the cottage, and very likely one or more indoors,
must have barked at the noise of the shooting. But
if any dim sense of the uproar did reach the keeper's
ear he put it down to the moon, at which dogs will
bay. As for his assistants, they had quietly gone
home, so soon as they felt sure that the keeper was
housed for the night. Long immunity from attack had
bred over-confidence ; the staff also was too small
for the extent of the place, and this had doubtless
become known. No one sleeps so soundly as an
agricultural labourer ; and as the nearest hamlet was
at some distance it is not surprising that they did not
wake.

In the early morning a fogger going to fodder his
cattle came across a pheasant lying dead on the
path, the snow stained with its blood. He picked it
up, and put it under his smock-frock, and carried it
to the pen, where he hid it under some litter, intend-
ing to take it home. But afterwards, as he crossed
the fields towards the farm, he passed near the wood
and observed the tracks of many feet and a gap in
the fence. He looked through the gap and saw that
the track went into the preserves. On second
thoughts he went back for the pheasant and took it
to his master.

The farmer, who was sitting down to table, quietly ate his breakfast, and then strolled over to the keeper's cottage with the bird.   This was the first intimation : the keeper could hardly believe it, till he himself went down and followed the trail of foot-marks.   There was not the least difficulty in tracing the course of the poachers through the wood ; the feathers were lying about ; the scorched paper (for they used muzzle-loaders), broken boughs, and shot-marks were all too plain.   But by this time the gang were well away, and none were captured or identified.

The extreme severity of the frost naturally caused people to stay indoors, so that no one noticed the cart going through the village ; nor could the track of its wheels be discerned from others on the snow of the highway beaten down firm.   Even had the poachers been disturbed, it is doubtful if so small a staff of keepers could have done anything to stop them.   As it was, they not only made a good haul —the largest made for years in that locality—but quite spoiled the shooting.

There are no white figures passing through the peaceful wood to-night and firing up into the trees. It is perfectly still.   The broad moon moves slow, and the bright rays light up tree and bush, so that it is easy to see through, except where the brambles retain their leaves and are fringed with the dead ferns.

The poaching of the present day is carried on with a few appliances only. An old-fashioned poacher could employ a variety of 'engines,' but the modern has scarcely any choice. There was, for instance, a very effective mode of setting a wire with a springe or bow. A stout stick was thrust into the ground, and then bent over into an arch. When the wire was thrown it instantly released the springe, which sprang up and drew it fast round the neck of the hare or rabbit, whose fore feet were lifted from the earth. Sometimes a growing sapling was bent down for the bow if it chanced to stand conveniently near a run. The hare no sooner put her head into the noose than she was suspended and strangled.

I tried the springe several times for rabbits, and found it answer; but the poacher cannot use it because it is so conspicuous. The stick itself, rising above the grass, is visible at some distance, and when thrown it holds the hare or rabbit up for any one to see that passes by. With a wire set in the present manner the captured animal lies extended, and often rolls into a furrow and is further hidden.

The springe was probably last employed by the mole-catchers. Their wooden traps were in the shape of a small tunnel, with a wire in the middle which, when the mole passed through, set free a bent stick. This stick pulled the wire and hung the mole. Such mole-catchers' bows or springes used to be seen in every meadow, but are now superseded by the iron trap.

Springes with horsehair nooses on the ground were also set for woodcocks and for wild ducks. It is said that a springe of somewhat similar construction was used for pheasants. Horsehair nooses are still applied for capturing woodpeckers and the owls that spend the day in hollow trees, being set round the hole by which they leave the tree. A more delicate horsehair noose is sometimes set for finches and small birds. I tried it for bullfinches, but did not succeed from lack of the dexterity required. The modes of using bird-lime were numerous, and many of them are in use for taking song-birds.

But the enclosure of open lands, the strict definition of footpaths, closer cultivation, and the increased value of game have so checked the poacher's operations with nets that in many districts the net may be said to be extinct. It is no longer necessary to bush the stubbles immediately after reaping. Brambles are said to have been the best for hindering the net, which frequently swept away an entire covey, old birds and young together. Stubbles are now so short that no birds will lie in them, and the net would not be successful there if it were tried.

The net used to be so favourite an 'engine' because partridges and pheasants will run rather than fly. In the case of partridges the poacher had first to ascertain the haunt of the covey, which he could do by looking for where they roost at night : the spot is often worn almost bare of grass and easily found. Or he could listen in the evening for the calling of the birds as they run together. The net being set, he walked very slowly down the wind towards the covey. It could not be done too quietly or gently, because if one got up all the rest would immediately take wing ; for partridges act in concert. If he took his time and let them run in front of him he secured the whole number.

That was the principle ; but the nets were of many kinds : the partridges were sometimes driven in by a dog. The partridges that appear in the market on the morning of the 1st of September are said to be netted, though probably by those who have a right to do so. These birds by nature lend themselves to such tricks, being so timid. It is said that if continually driven to and fro they will at last cower, and can be taken by hand or knocked over with a stick.

The sight of a paper kite in the air makes them motionless till forced to rise ; and there was an old dodge of ringing a bell at night, which so alarmed the covey that they remained still till the net was ready, when a sudden flash of light drove them into it. Imagine a poacher ringing a bell nowadays ! Then, partridges were peculiarly liable to be taken ; now, perhaps, they escape better than any other kind of game. Except with a gun the poacher can hardly touch them, and after the coveys have been broken up it is not worth his while to risk a shot very often. If only their eggs could be protected there should be little difficulty with partridges.

Pheasants are more individual in their ways, and act less together ; but they have the same habit of running instead of flying, and if a poacher did but dare he could take them with nets as easily as possible. They form runs through the woods—just as fowls will wander day after day down a hedge, till they have made quite a path. So that, having found the run and knowing the position of the birds, the rest is simplicity itself. The net being stretched, the pheasants were driven in. A cur dog was sometimes sent round to disturb the birds. Being a cur, he did not bark, for which reason a strain of cur is preferred to this day by the mouchers who keep dogs. Now that the woods are regularly watched such a plan has become impracticable. It might indeed be done once, but surely not twice where competent keepers were about.

Nets were also used for hares and rabbits, which were driven in by a dog ; but, the scent of these animals being so good, it was necessary to work in such a manner that the wind might not blow from the net, meeting them as they approached it. Pheasants, as every one knows, roost on trees, but often do not ascend very high ; and, indeed, before the leaves are off they are said to be sometimes taken by hand— sliding it along the bough till the legs are grasped, just as you might fowls perched at night on a rail across the beams of a shed.

The spot where they roost is easily found out, because of the peculiar noise they make upon flying up ; and with a little precaution the trees may be approached without startling them. Years ago the poacher carried a sulphur match and lit it under the tree, when the fumes, ascending, stupefied the birds, which fell to the ground. The process strongly resembled the way in which old-fashioned folk stifled their bees by placing the hive at night, when the insects were still, over a piece of brown paper dipped in molten brimstone and ignited. The apparently

dead bees were afterwards shaken out and buried ; but
upon moving the earth with a spade some of them
would crawl out, even after two or three days.

Sulphur fumes were likewise used for compelling
rabbits to bolt from their buries without a ferret.   I
tried an experiment in a bury once with a mixture the
chief component of which was gunpowder, so managed
as to burn slowly and give a great smoke.   The rabbits did, indeed, just hop out and hop in again ; but it
is a most clumsy expedient, because the fire must be
lit on the windward side, and the rabbits will only
come out to leeward.   The smoke hangs, and does
not penetrate into half the tunnels ; or else it blows
through quickly, when you must stop half the holes
with a spade.   It is a wretched substitute for a ferret.

When cock-fighting was common the bellicose
inclinations of the cock-pheasants were sometimes
excited to their destruction.   A game-cock was first
armed with the sharp spur made from the best razors,
and then put down near where a pheasant-cock had
been observed to crow.   The pheasant-cock is so
thoroughly game that he will not allow any rival
crowing in his locality, and the two quickly met in
battle.   Like a keen poniard the game-cock's spur
either slew the pheasant outright or got fixed in the
pheasant's feathers, when he was captured.

A pheasant, too, as he ran deeper into the wood upon an alarm, occasionally found his neck in a noose suspended across his path. For rabbiting, the lurcher was and is the dog of all others. He is as cunning and wily in approaching his game as if he had a cross of feline nature in his character. Other dogs trust to speed ; but the lurcher steals on his prey without a sound. He enters into the purpose of his master, and if any one appears in sight remains quietly in the hedge with the rabbit or leveret in his mouth till a sign bids him approach. If half the stories told of the docility and intelligence of the lurcher are true, the poacher needs no other help than one of these dogs for ground game. But the dogs called lurchers nowadays are mostly of degenerate and impure breed ; still, even these are capable of a good deal.

There is a way of fishing with rod and line, but without a bait. The rod should be in one piece, or else a stout one—the line also very strong and short, the hook of large size. When the fish is discovered the hook is quietly dropped into the water and allowed to float, in seeming, along, till close under it. The rod is then jerked up, and the barb enters the body of the fish and drags it out.

This plan requires, of course, that the fish should be

visible, and if stationary is more easily practised ; but it is also effective even against small fish that swim together in large shoals, for if the hook misses one it strikes another.   The most fatal time for fish is when they spawn : roach, jack, and trout alike are then within reach, and if the poacher dares to visit the water he is certain of a haul.

Even in the present day and in the south a fawn is now and then stolen from parks and forests where deer are kept.   Being small, it is not much more difficult to hide than a couple of hares ; and once in the carrier's cart and at a little distance no one asks any questions.   Such game always finds a ready sale ; and when a savoury dish is on the table those who are about to eat it do not inquire whence it came any more than the old folk did centuries ago. A nod and a wink are the best sauce. As the keepers are allowed to sell a certain number of fawns (or say they are), it is not possible for any one at a distance to know whether the game was poached or not. An ordinary single-barrel muzzle-loader of the commonest kind with a charge of common shot will kill a fawn.

I once started to stalk a pheasant that was feeding in the corner of a meadow. Beyond the meadow there was a cornfield which extended across to a preserved wood. But the open stubble afforded no cover—any one walking in it could be seen—so that the pheasant had to be got at from one side only. It was necessary also that he should be shot dead without fluttering of wings, the wood being so near.

The afternoon sun, shining in a cloudless sky—it was a still October day—beat hot against the western side of the hedge as I noiselessly walked beside it. In the aftermath, green but flowerless, a small flock of sheep were feeding—one with a long briar clinging to his wool. They moved slowly before me ; a thing I wanted ; for behind sheep almost any game can be approached.

I have also frequently shot rabbits that were out feeding, by the aid of a herd of cows. It does not seem to be so much the actual cover as the scent of the animals ; for a man of course can be seen over sheep, and under the legs of cattle. But the breath and odour of sheep or cows prevent the game from scenting him, and, what is equally effective, the cattle, to which they are accustomed, throw them off their guard.

The cart-horses in the fields do not answer so well : if you try to use one for stalking, unless he knows you he will sheer off and set up a clumsy gallop, being afraid of capture and a return to work. But cows will feed steadily in front ; and a flock of

sheep, very slowly driven, move on with a gentle
'tinkle, tinkle.' Wild creatures show no fear of what
they are accustomed to, and the use of which they
understand.

If a solitary hurdle be set up in a meadow as a
hiding-place from behind which to shoot the rabbits
of a burrow, not one will come out within gun-shot
that evening. They know that it is something strange,
the use of which they do not understand and therefore
avoid. When I first began to shoot, the difficulty
was to judge the distances, and to know how far a
rabbit was from a favourite hiding-place. I once
carefully dropped small green boughs, just broken
off, at twenty, thirty, and forty yards, measuring by
paces. This was in the morning.

In the evening not a rabbit would come out any-
where near these boughs; they were shy of them
even when the leaves had withered and turned brown;
so that I took them away. Yet of the green boughs
blown off by a gale, or the dead grey branches that
fall of their own weight, they take no notice.

First, then, they must have heard me in their
burrows pacing by; secondly, they scented the
boughs as having been handled, and connected the
two circumstances together and, thirdly, though
aware that the boughs themselves were harmless, they

felt that harm was intended. The pheasant had been walking about in the corner where the hedges met, but now he went in ; still, as he entered the hedge in a quiet way, he did not appear to be alarmed. The sheep, tired of being constantly driven from their food, now sheered out from the hedge, and allowed me to go by.

As I passed I gathered a few haws and ate them. The reason why birds do not care much for berries before they are forced to take to them by frost is because of the stone within, so that the food afforded by the berries is really small. Yew-berries are an exception ; they have a stone, but the covering to it is sweet, succulent, and thick, and dearly loved by thrushes. In the ditch the tall grasses, having escaped the scythe, bowed low with the weight of their own awn-like seeds.

The corner was not far off now ; and I waited awhile behind a large hawthorn bush growing on the 'shore' of the ditch, thinking that I might see the pheasant on the mound, or that at least he would recover confidence if he had previously heard anything. Inside the bush was a nest already partly filled with fallen leaves, like a little basket.

A rabbit had been feeding on the other side, but now, suspicious, came over the bank, and, seeing me,

suddenly stopped and lifted himself up. In that
moment I could have shot him, being so near,
without putting the gun to the shoulder, by the sense
of direction in the hands; the next he dived into a
burrow.   Looking round the bush, I now saw the
pheasant in the hedge that crossed at right angles in
front; this was fortunate, because through that hedge
there was another meadow.   It was full of nut-tree
bushes, very tall and thick at the top, but lower
down thin, as is usually the case when poles grow
high.   To fill the space a fence had been made of
stakes and bushes woven between them, and on this
the pheasant stood.

It was too far for a safe shot; in a minute he
went down into the meadow on the other side.   I
then crept on hands and knees towards the nut-
bushes: as I got nearer there was a slight rustle and
a low hiss in the grass, and I had to pause while a
snake went by hastening for the ditch.   A few
moments afterwards, being close to the hedge, I
rose partly up, and looked carefully over the fence
between the hazel wands.   There was the pheasant
not fifteen yards away, his back somewhat towards
me, and quietly questing about.

In lifting the gun I had to push aside a bough—
the empty hoods from which a bunch of brown nuts

had fallen rested against the barrel as I looked along it. I aimed at the head—knowing that it would mean instant death, and would also avoid shattering the bird at so short a range ; besides which there would be fewer scattered feathers to collect and thrust out of sight into a rabbit bury. A reason why people frequently miss pheasants in cover-shooting, despite of their size, is because they look at the body, the wings, and the tail. But if they looked only at the head, and thought of that, very few would escape. My finger felt the trigger, and the least increase of pressure would have been fatal ; but in the act I hesitated, dropped the barrel, and watched the beautiful bird.

That watching so often stayed the shot that at last it grew to be a habit : the mere simple pleasure of seeing birds and animals, when they were quite unconscious that they were observed, being too great to be spoiled by the discharge. After carefully getting a wire over a jack ; after waiting in a tree till a hare came along ; after sitting in a mound till the partridges began to run together to roost ; in the end the wire or gun remained unused. The same feeling has equally checked my hand in legitimate shooting : time after time I have flushed partridges without firing, and have let the hare bound over the furrow free.

I have entered many woods just for the pleasure
of creeping through the brake and the thickets.
Destruction in itself was not the motive ; it was an
overpowering instinct for woods and fields. Yet
woods and fields lose half their interest without a gun
—I like the power to shoot, even though I may not
use it. The very perfection of our modern guns is to
me one of their drawbacks : the use of them is so
easy and so certain of effect that it takes away the
romance of sport.

There could be no greater pleasure to me than to
wander with a matchlock through one of the great
forests or wild tracts that still remain in England. A
hare a day, a brace of partridges, or a wild duck would
be ample in the way of actual shooting. The weapon
itself, whether matchlock, wheel-lock, or even a crossbow, would be a delight. Some of the antique wheel-
lock guns are really beautiful specimens of design. The
old powder-horns are often gems of workmanship—
hunting scenes cut out in ivory, and the minutest
detail of hoof or antler rendered with life-like accuracy.
How pleasant these carvings feel to the fingers ! It
is delightful to handle such weapons and such implements.

The matchlocks, too, are inlaid or the stocks
carved. There is slaughter in every line of our modern

guns—mechanical slaughter. But were I offered par-
ticipation in the bloodiest battue ever arranged, or the
freedom of an English forest or mountain tract, to go
forth at any time untrammelled by attendant, but
only to shoot with matchlock, wheel-lock, or crossbow, my choice would be unhesitating.

There would be pleasure in winding up the lock
with the spanner ; pleasure in adjusting the priming ;
or with the matchlock in lighting the match. To
wander out into the brake, to creep from tree to tree
so noiselessly that the woodpecker should not cease
to tap—in that there is joy. The consciousness that
everything depends upon your own personal skill, and
that you have no second resource if that fails you,
gives the real zest to sport.

If the wheel did not knock a spark out quickly ; if
the priming had not been kept dry or the match not
properly blown, or the crossbow set exactly accurate,
then the care of approach would be lost. You must
hold the gun steady, too, while the slow priming
ignites the charge.

An imperfect weapon—yes ; but the imperfect
weapon would accord with the great oaks, the beech
trees full of knot-holes, the mysterious thickets, the
tall fern, the silence and the solitude. The chase
would become a real chase : not, as now, a foregone

conclusion.   And there would be time for pondering and dreaming.

Let us be always out of doors among trees and grass, and rain and wind and sun.   There the breeze comes and strikes the cheek and sets it aglow : the gale increases and the trees creak and roar, but it is only a ruder music.   A calm follows, the sun shines in the sky, and it is the time to sit under an oak, leaning against the bark, while the birds sing and the air is soft and sweet.   By night the stars shine, and there is no fathoming the dark spaces between those brilliant points, nor the thoughts that come as it were between the fixed stars and landmarks of the mind.

Or it is the morning on the hills, when hope is as wide as the world ; or it is the evening on the shore. A red sun sinks, and the foam-tipped waves are crested with crimson ; the booming surge breaks, and the spray flies afar, sprinkling the face watching under the pale cliffs.   Let us get out of these indoor narrow modern days, whose twelve hours somehow have become shortened, into the sunlight and the pure wind.   A something that the ancients called divine can be found and felt there still.